2019.

Dear Lyn

Happy Birthday.
Wishing you many
happy hours using this
book.

Love,

Mum.

COOK'S COLLECTION

SLOW COOKER

Fuss-free and tasty recipe ideas
for the modern cook

CONTENTS

INTRODUCTION

Slow cookers, believe it or not, are the solution for anyone wanting to save time in the kitchen. Dismiss any concerns about complicated and lengthy preparation because these handy low-tech appliances will actually save you time and still deliver unbeatable results.

What could be better than to arrive home after a long day to be greeted by the enticing aroma of a ready-to-eat, home-cooked meal? With a little preparation, chopping and sautéing, the hard work is done. The slow cooker then takes over and works its magic, transforming these ingredients into flavoursome meals, so you are set free from the kitchen.

Slow-cooked winter warmers have been enjoyed for years, so it's no surprise that the slow cooker is perfect for making flavour-packed soups and for turning economical cuts of meat into rich stews.

But it's not all comforting stews and warming soups, with recipes that range from a sunny frittata to fiery burritos, you can eat a different meal every night of the week, making the slow cooker the most versatile appliance in your kitchen.

And there's no need to pack away the slow cooker during the warmer months either. The mighty slow cooker is also great for cooking more delicate meats, fish and vegetables, because the ingredients are cooked gently without being broken down. Red Thai Curry with Salmon & Lime (see page 120) is a perfect, light meal that can be enjoyed all year round. As an added bonus, the slow cooker won't add extra heat to your kitchen.

It's a healthy way to cook too. The long cooking time simmers food in its own juices with no evaporation, so it keeps more vitamins and minerals than with conventional cooking, transforming dried beans and root vegetables into wholesome meals. More surprisingly, the slow cooker can be used to cook cakes and other desserts. The slow cooker makes light work of desserts to accompany any main meal, like Sweet Potato, Apple &

Raisin Compote (see page 177). So if you're short of oven space for dinner, the slow cooker offers the extra help you need.

There are a wide variety of types and sizes of slow cooker available, so have a look and choose the one that's right for you. A 3.8-litre/6½-pint slow cooker is ideal for a family of four or five, while a 1.9-litre/3¼-pint cooker might be perfect for a couple. Larger cookers are great for large families, people who entertain or those who like to cook a big dish and freeze leftovers. Many recipes here can be prepared in a 1.9-litre/3¼-pint slow cooker, but some slow cookers may need liquid volumes adjusted where ingredients need to be covered.

Preparation is as key with the slow cooker as it is with any other type of cooking. Some ingredients may need a bit of sautéing or frying before they're added to the pot. Onions, leeks and garlic are a good example – you can add them to the pot without pre-cooking them, but bringing them to the soft translucent stage will make all the difference to the flavour of your finished dish. If you don't have a lot of time in the mornings, prep all your ingredients the night before, put them in the slow cooker pot and place in the fridge overnight, then leave the pot to stand at room temperature for 20 minutes the following morning before switching on the slow cooker.

When you're layering your ingredients in the pot for a meat stew or casserole, remember to put the root vegetables in first – they take longest to cook, and the base of the slow cooker, nearest the heating element, is the hottest part.

A word of warning for cooking dried beans. Dried beans cooked in the slow cooker have been linked to food poisoning. To eliminate this risk, soak dried beans for at least 5 hours prior to cooking, and then drain and rinse them, place them in a saucepan, cover with cold water, bring to the boil over a medium–high heat and cook at a rapid boil for at least 10 minutes. Remove from the heat, rinse and drain one more time, and then place the beans in the slow cooker, cover with at least 2.5 cm/1 inch of cold water and cook on low, covered, for about 8–10 hours, until tender. To prevent the beans becoming tough, do not add salt until after cooking.

A few of the recipes in this book need a metal trivet. This is sometimes useful when you are baking bread or cakes, or when roasting a chicken so that the chicken doesn't sit on the base of the slow cooker and become scorched. Some slow cookers come with a trivet. If yours doesn't, then you can use aluminium foil shaped into balls or into a ring to support the ingredient. Other options for slow cooker trivets are a metal canning ring or a large onion cut into big chunks to support the baking container or ingredient.

Try to resist the temptation to lift the lid and see how things are getting on. The cooker will lose a lot of heat and it will take a while for it to reach the right temperature again. Don't stint on the slow cooking times either. The longer and slower your food cooks, the more time it has to develop the depth of flavour that makes it so delicious.

Once you start using your slow cooker to cook the wide variety of delicious recipes in this book you'll probably begin to wonder if you'll ever use your conventional oven again. So, what are you waiting for? Dust off your slow cooker and get cooking!

CHAPTER ONE

· · · · ✕ · · · ·

VEGETARIAN

· · ·

BLACK BEAN CHILLI WITH SMOKED CHIPOTLE & RED PEPPER

SERVES: *4* | PREP: *25 mins, plus soaking* | COOK: *8 hours*

INGREDIENTS

250 g/9 oz dried black beans,
  soaked in cold water overnight,
  or for at least 5 hours
500 ml/18 fl oz boiling water
1 dried chipotle chilli
2 onions, sliced
3 garlic cloves, sliced
1 tsp ground cumin
1 tsp smoked paprika
500 g/1 lb 2 oz passata
1 tbsp tomato purée
3 red peppers, deseeded and sliced
1 large courgette, sliced
1 avocado, sliced, to garnish
2 tbsp chopped fresh coriander, to
  garnish
4 tbsp soured cream, to serve

1. Drain and rinse the beans, place in a saucepan, cover with fresh cold water and bring to the boil. Boil rapidly for at least 10 minutes, then remove from the heat, drain and rinse again.

2. Pour the boiling water over the chilli and leave to soak for 5 minutes. Remove the chilli from the water, reserving the liquid, and finely slice the chilli.

3. Put the chilli, onions, garlic, cumin, paprika, beans, passata, tomato purée, red peppers and courgette into the slow cooker. Add the reserved chipotle water, cover the slow cooker and cook on low for 8 hours.

4. Transfer to warmed plates, garnish each serving with avocado and coriander and serve with a tablespoon of soured cream on top.

CAVOLO NERO, GOAT'S CHEESE & SUN-DRIED TOMATO FRITTATA

SERVES: *4* | PREP: *15 mins* | COOK: *3 hours 10 mins*

INGREDIENTS

1 tbsp olive oil, plus extra for brushing

1 onion, roughly chopped

3 garlic cloves, roughly chopped

200 g/7 oz cavolo nero, shredded

8 eggs, beaten

8 sun-dried tomatoes, drained and roughly chopped

2 tbsp roughly chopped fresh parsley

100 g/3½ oz vegetarian goat's cheese, crumbled

salt and pepper (optional)

1. Heat the oil in a large frying pan over a medium heat. Add the onion and cook over a low heat, stirring occasionally, for 3–4 minutes until soft. Add the garlic and cavolo nero and cook for a further 5 minutes.

2. Meanwhile, stir the eggs, sun-dried tomatoes, parsley and half the goat's cheese through the onion mixture. Season well with salt and pepper, if using.

3. Lightly brush the inside of the slow cooker with oil and pour in the frittata mixture. Crumble the remaining goat's cheese over the surface of the frittata.

4. Cover the slow cooker and cook on low for 2½–3 hours, or until the frittata is set and beginning to brown at the edges. Serve warm, or leave to cool.

ITALIAN BREAD
SOUP WITH GREENS

SERVES: *4* | **PREP:** *20 mins* | **COOK:** *4 hours 35 mins–8 hours 35 mins*

INGREDIENTS

2 tbsp olive oil

1 onion, diced

1 leek, halved lengthways and
*   thinly sliced*

2 litres/3½ pints vegetable stock

200 g/7 oz kale, chopped

2 celery sticks, diced

2 carrots, diced

1 tsp crumbled dried oregano

1½ tsp salt

½ tsp pepper

200 g/7 oz day-old cubed
*   sourdough bread*

25 g/1 oz freshly grated Parmesan-
*   style vegetarian cheese, to*
*   garnish*

1. Heat the oil in a large frying pan over a medium–high heat. Add the onion and leek and sauté for about 5 minutes until soft.

2. Transfer the mixture to the slow cooker and add the stock, kale, celery, carrots, oregano, salt and pepper. Cover and cook on high for about 4 hours or on low for 8 hours.

3. Add the bread to the soup, re-cover and cook on high, stirring occasionally, for about 30 minutes, until the bread breaks down and thickens the soup.

4. Serve immediately, garnished with the cheese.

GREEK BEAN &
VEGETABLE SOUP

SERVES: *4–6* | **PREP:** *25 mins, plus soaking* | **COOK:** *12 hours 20 mins*

INGREDIENTS

500g/1 lb 2 oz dried haricot beans,
soaked in cold water overnight,
or for at least 5 hours
2 onions, finely chopped
2 garlic cloves, finely chopped
2 potatoes, chopped
2 carrots, chopped
2 tomatoes, peeled and chopped
2 celery sticks, chopped
4 tbsp extra virgin olive oil
1 bay leaf
2 litres/3½ pints boiling water
salt and pepper (optional)
12 black olives, stoned and sliced,
and 2 tbsp snipped fresh chives,
to garnish

1. Drain the beans and rinse well under cold running water. Place the beans in a saucepan, cover with cold water and bring to the boil. Boil rapidly for at least 10 minutes, then remove from the heat, drain and rinse again.

2. Place the beans in the slow cooker and add the onions, garlic, potatoes, carrots, tomatoes, celery, olive oil and bay leaf.

3. Pour in 2 litres/3½ pints of boiling water, making sure that all the ingredients are fully submerged. Cover and cook on low for 12 hours until the beans are tender.

4. Remove and discard the bay leaf. Season the soup to taste with salt and pepper, if using, and garnish with the olives and chives. Transfer to warmed soup bowls and serve immediately.

STUFFED BUTTERNUT SQUASH

SERVES: *4* | **PREP:** *25 mins* | **COOK:** *6 hours 35 mins*

INGREDIENTS

2 tbsp olive oil

1 shallot, diced

2 garlic cloves, finely chopped

250 g/9 oz chard, stems and thick centre ribs removed and leaves cut into wide ribbons

¾ tsp salt

1 tsp paprika

450 ml/16 fl oz vegetable stock

175 g/6 oz quinoa

425 g/15 oz canned cannellini beans, rinsed and drained

25 g/1 oz stoned Kalamata olives, diced

115 g/4 oz vegetarian feta cheese, crumbled

2 tbsp finely chopped fresh mint leaves

2 butternut squash, halved and deseeded

1. Heat the oil in a large frying pan over a medium–high heat. Add the shallot and garlic and cook, stirring, for about 5 minutes until soft. Add the chard and cook for about 3 minutes until wilted. Add the salt and paprika and cook for a further 1 minute. Add the stock and quinoa and bring to the boil. Reduce the heat to low, cover and simmer for 15–20 minutes, until the quinoa is cooked through.

2. Stir in the beans, olives, half the cheese and the mint.

3. Fill the slow cooker with water to a depth of 5 mm/¼ inch. Divide the quinoa mixture between the squash halves, then place them in the slow cooker stuffed side up. Cover and cook on low for 6 hours.

4. Preheat the grill. Remove the squash from the slow cooker and top with the remaining cheese. Cook under the preheated grill for 3 minutes until the cheese is beginning to brown. Serve immediately.

WINTER VEGETABLE MEDLEY

SERVES: *4* | **PREP:** *15–20 mins* | **COOK:** *3 hours 30 mins*

INGREDIENTS

2 tbsp sunflower oil
2 onions, chopped
3 carrots, chopped
3 parsnips, chopped
2 bunches celery, chopped
2 tbsp chopped fresh parsley
1 tbsp chopped fresh coriander
300 ml/10 fl oz vegetable stock
salt and pepper (optional)

1. Heat the oil in a large, heavy-based saucepan. Add the onions and cook over a medium heat, stirring occasionally, for 5 minutes until soft.

2. Add the carrots, parsnips and celery and cook, stirring occasionally, for a further 5 minutes.

3. Stir in the herbs, season with salt and pepper, if using, and pour in the stock. Bring to the boil.

4. Transfer the vegetable mixture to the slow cooker, cover and cook on high for 3 hours until tender. Taste and adjust the seasoning, if using.

5. Using a slotted spoon, transfer the medley to warmed plates, then spoon over a little of the cooking liquid. Serve immediately.

SPAGHETTI WITH LENTIL BOLOGNESE SAUCE

SERVES: *4–6* | **PREP:** *20 mins* | **COOK:** *8 hours 15 mins*

INGREDIENTS

2 tbsp olive oil

1 onion, diced

2 garlic cloves, finely chopped

1 carrot, diced

2 celery sticks, diced

4 large mushrooms, diced

1 tbsp tomato purée

1 tsp salt

1 tsp crumbled dried oregano

1 bay leaf

400 g/14 oz canned chopped tomatoes, with juice

50 g/1¾ oz dried lentils

225 ml/8 fl oz water

450 g/1 lb dried spaghetti

1. Heat the oil in a large frying pan over a medium–high heat. Add the onion and garlic and cook, stirring, for about 5 minutes until soft. Add the carrot, celery and mushrooms and continue to cook, stirring occasionally, for a further 5 minutes, or until the mushrooms are soft. Stir in the tomato purée, salt, oregano and bay leaf and cook, stirring, for a further 1 minute. Transfer the mixture to the slow cooker.

2. Stir in the tomatoes with their can juices, the lentils and water. Cover and cook on high for 8 hours.

3. Just before serving, cook the spaghetti according to the packet instructions. Transfer the spaghetti to warmed serving dishes and spoon the hot sauce over. Serve immediately.

SWEET & SOUR SICILIAN PASTA

SERVES: *4* | **PREP:** *25 mins* | **COOK:** *5 hours 20 mins*

INGREDIENTS

4 tbsp olive oil

1 large red onion, sliced

2 garlic cloves, finely chopped

2 red peppers, deseeded and sliced

2 courgettes, cut into batons

1 aubergine, cut into batons

450 ml/16 fl oz passata

150 ml/5 fl oz water

4 tbsp lemon juice

2 tbsp balsamic vinegar

55 g/2 oz stoned black olives, sliced

1 tbsp sugar

400 g/14 oz dried pappardelle

salt and pepper (optional)

4 fresh flat-leaf parsley sprigs, to garnish

1. Heat the oil in a large, heavy-based saucepan. Add the onion, garlic and red peppers and cook over a low heat, stirring occasionally, for 5 minutes. Add the courgettes and aubergine and cook, stirring occasionally, for a further 5 minutes. Stir in the passata and water and bring to the boil. Stir in the lemon juice, vinegar, olives and sugar and season to taste with salt and pepper, if using.

2. Transfer the mixture to the slow cooker. Cover and cook on low for 5 hours until all the vegetables are tender.

3. Before serving, cook the pasta. Add a little salt, if using, to a large saucepan of water and bring to the boil. Add the pasta, bring back to the boil and cook for 10–12 minutes until the pasta is tender but still firm to the bite. Drain and transfer to a warmed serving dish. Spoon the vegetable mixture over the pasta, lightly toss, garnish with parsley and serve.

VEGETABLE PASTA

SERVES: *4* | **PREP:** *20 mins* | **COOK:** *3 hours 25 mins*

INGREDIENTS

250 g/9 oz dried penne
2 tbsp olive oil, plus extra
* for drizzling*
1 red onion, sliced
2 courgettes, thinly sliced
200 g/7 oz closed-cup mushrooms,
* sliced*
2 tbsp chopped fresh oregano
300 g/10½ oz tomatoes, sliced
55 g/2 oz freshly grated Parmesan-
* style vegetarian cheese*
salt and pepper (optional)

1. Add a little salt, if using, to a large saucepan of water and bring to the boil. Add the pasta, bring back to the boil and cook for 8–10 minutes, or until tender but still firm to the bite. Drain. Meanwhile, heat the oil in a heavy-based saucepan, add the onion and cook over a medium heat, stirring occasionally, for 5 minutes until soft. Stir into the pasta.

2. Place a layer of courgettes and mushrooms in the slow cooker and top with a layer of pasta. Sprinkle with oregano, and salt and pepper, if using, and continue layering, finishing with a layer of vegetables.

3. Arrange the sliced tomatoes on top and drizzle with oil. Cover and cook on high for 3 hours, or until tender.

4. Sprinkle with cheese, re-cover and cook for a further 10 minutes. Transfer to a warmed serving bowl and serve immediately.

PUMPKIN RISOTTO

SERVES: *4* | **PREP:** *20 mins* | **COOK:** *1 hour 55 mins*

INGREDIENTS

2 tbsp olive oil

1 shallot, finely chopped

1 garlic clove, finely chopped

280 g/10 oz arborio rice

125 ml/4 fl oz vegetarian dry white wine

1.2 litres/2 pints vegetable stock

425 g/15 oz canned pumpkin purée

1 tbsp finely chopped fresh sage

½ tsp salt

¼ tsp pepper

pinch of nutmeg

2 tbsp butter

115 g/4 oz freshly grated Parmesan-style vegetarian cheese, plus extra to serve

1. Heat the oil in a large frying pan over a medium–high heat. Add the shallot and garlic and cook, stirring, for about 5 minutes, until soft. Add the rice and cook, stirring, for 1 minute. Add the wine and cook for a further 3 minutes until the liquid is absorbed. Transfer the mixture to the slow cooker.

2. Stir in the stock, pumpkin purée, sage, salt, pepper and nutmeg. Cover and cook on high for about 1½ hours until the rice is tender. Stir in the butter, re-cover and cook for a further 15 minutes. Stir in the cheese and serve immediately, with a little cheese sprinkled over.

ASPARAGUS & SPINACH RISOTTO

SERVES: *4* | **PREP:** *20 mins* | **COOK:** *2 hours 35 mins*

INGREDIENTS

2 tbsp olive oil

4 shallots, finely chopped

280 g/10 oz arborio rice

1 garlic clove, crushed

*100 ml/3½ fl oz vegetarian dry
    white wine*

850 ml/1½ pints vegetable stock

200 g/7 oz asparagus spears

200 g/7 oz baby spinach leaves

*40 g/1½ oz freshly grated
    Parmesan-style vegetarian
    cheese*

salt and pepper (optional)

1. Heat the oil in a frying pan, add the shallots and fry over a medium heat, stirring, for 2–3 minutes. Add the rice and garlic and cook for a further 2 minutes, stirring constantly. Add the wine and allow to boil for 30 seconds.

2. Transfer the rice mixture to the slow cooker, add the stock and season to taste with salt and pepper, if using. Cover and cook on high for 2 hours, or until most of the liquid is absorbed.

3. Cut the asparagus into 4-cm/1½-inch lengths. Stir into the rice, then spread the spinach over the top. Re-cover and cook on high for a further 30 minutes, until the asparagus is just tender and the spinach is wilted.

4. Stir in the cheese, then adjust the seasoning to taste, if using, and serve immediately in warmed bowls.

MACARONI CHEESE WITH TOASTED BREADCRUMBS

SERVES: 4 | **PREP:** 20 mins | **COOK:** 2 hours 20 mins–4 hours 20 mins

INGREDIENTS

vegetable oil, for brushing
2 tbsp butter
2 tbsp plain flour
150 ml/5 fl oz vegetable stock
450 ml/16 fl oz evaporated milk
1½ tsp mustard powder
⅛–¼ tsp cayenne pepper
1 tsp salt
175 g/6 oz vegetarian Gruyère
   cheese, grated
175 g/6 oz vegetarian fontina
   cheese, grated
55 g/2 oz freshly grated Parmesan-
   style vegetarian cheese
350 g/12 oz dried elbow macaroni
350 ml/12 fl oz water

TOPPING

2 thick slices French bread or
   sourdough bread
2 tbsp butter

1. Line the slow cooker with foil and brush with a little oil.

2. Melt the butter in a large frying pan or saucepan over a medium–high heat. Whisk in the flour and cook for 1 minute. Reduce the heat to medium and slowly add the stock, evaporated milk, mustard powder, cayenne pepper and salt. Cook, stirring, for about 3–5 minutes until thick. Add all the cheeses and whisk until melted. Add the macaroni and stir to mix well. Transfer to the slow cooker.

3. Add the water and stir to mix. Cover and cook on high for about 2 hours or on low for about 4 hours until the macaroni is tender.

4. To make the topping, process the bread in a food processor to make crumbs. Melt the butter in a large frying pan over a medium heat until bubbling. Add the breadcrumbs and cook, stirring frequently, for about 5 minutes until toasted and golden brown.

5. Serve immediately topped with the breadcrumbs.

AUBERGINE TIMBALES

SERVES: *4* | **PREP:** *25 mins* | **COOK:** *2 hours 30 mins*

INGREDIENTS

2 aubergines

3 tbsp olive oil, plus extra for oiling

2 onions, finely chopped

2 red peppers, deseeded and
  chopped

1 large tomato, peeled and chopped

6 tbsp milk

2 egg yolks

¼ tsp ground cinnamon

85 g/3 oz crispbread, crushed

300 ml/10 fl oz soured cream

salt and pepper (optional)

4 fresh flat-leaf parsley sprigs,
  to garnish

1. Halve the aubergines and scoop out the flesh. Reserve the shells and dice the flesh. Heat the oil in a large, heavy-based frying pan. Add the onions and cook over a low heat for 5 minutes. Add the diced aubergines, red peppers and tomato and cook, stirring occasionally, for 15–20 minutes until all the vegetables are soft. Remove the pan from the heat.

2. Transfer the mixture to a food processor or blender and process to a purée, then scrape into a bowl. Beat together the milk, egg yolks and cinnamon in a jug. Season with salt and pepper, if using, then stir into the vegetable purée.

3. Brush four ramekins or cups with oil and sprinkle with enough of the crispbread crumbs to coat. Tip out any excess. Mix about three quarters of the remaining crumbs into the vegetable purée. Slice the aubergine shells into strips and use them to line the ramekins, leaving the ends overlapping the rims. Spoon the filling into the ramekins, sprinkle with the remaining crumbs and fold over the overlapping ends of the aubergine. Cover the ramekins with foil.

4. Stand the ramekins on a trivet or rack in the slow cooker and pour in enough boiling water to come about one third of the way up the sides of the ramekins. Cover and cook on high for 2 hours.

5. To make the sauce, lightly beat the soured cream and season with salt and pepper, if using. Lift the ramekins out of the slow cooker and remove the foil. Invert onto serving plates, garnish with parsley sprigs and serve immediately with the sauce.

WHITE BEAN
STEW

SERVES: *4* | **PREP:** *25 mins* | **COOK:** *3 hours 20 mins–6 hours 20 mins*

INGREDIENTS

2 tbsp olive oil

1 onion, diced

2 garlic cloves, finely chopped

2 carrots, diced

2 celery sticks, diced

175 g/6 oz canned tomato purée

1 tsp salt

½ tsp pepper

*¼–½ tsp crushed dried red pepper
    flakes*

1 bay leaf

*225 ml/8 fl oz vegetarian dry white
    wine*

*850 g/1 lb 14 oz canned cannellini
    beans, rinsed and drained*

*250 g/9 oz chard, kale or other
    winter greens, stems and thick
    centre ribs removed, leaves cut
    into wide ribbons*

225 ml/8 fl oz water

*25 g/1 oz freshly grated Parmesan-
    style vegetarian cheese, to serve*

1. Heat the oil in a large frying pan over a medium–high heat. Add the onion and garlic and cook, stirring, for about 5 minutes until soft. Add the carrots and celery and cook for a further few minutes. Stir in the tomato purée, salt, pepper, red pepper flakes and bay leaf, then add the wine.

2. Bring to the boil and cook, stirring and scraping up any sediment from the base of the pan, for about 5 minutes until most of the liquid has evaporated. Transfer the mixture to the slow cooker.

3. Stir in the beans, chard and water. Cover and cook on high for 3 hours or on low for 6 hours. Remove and discard the bay leaf. Serve the stew hot, garnished with the cheese.

BUTTERNUT SQUASH &
GOAT'S CHEESE ENCHILADAS

SERVES: *4* | **PREP:** *35–40 mins* | **COOK:** *2 hours 50 mins–3 hours*

INGREDIENTS

*1 large butternut squash, peeled
  and diced*
4 tbsp olive oil
1 tsp salt
3 tsp ground cumin
1 large onion, diced
3 garlic cloves, finely chopped
1 tbsp hot or mild chilli powder
1 tbsp dried oregano
450g/1 lb passata
1 tbsp clear honey
450 ml/16 fl oz vegetable stock
12 corn tortillas
*225 g/8 oz soft, fresh vegetarian
  goat's cheese*

1. Preheat the oven to 200°C/400°F/Gas Mark 6. Line a baking tray or dish with baking paper. Coat the squash with 2 tablespoons of the oil, sprinkle with half the salt and 1 teaspoon of the cumin. Place the squash on the prepared tray and roast in the preheated oven for 30–40 minutes until soft and beginning to brown.

2. Heat the remaining oil in a large frying pan over a medium–high heat. Add the onion and garlic and cook, stirring, for about 5 minutes until soft. Add the remaining cumin and salt, the chilli powder and the oregano and cook for a further 1 minute. Stir in the passata, honey and stock, bring to the boil and cook for about 5 minutes. Purée the sauce in a food processor or blender.

3. Coat the base of the slow cooker with a little sauce. Make a layer of tortillas, tearing them if necessary, to cover the base of the slow cooker. Top the tortillas with a layer of the squash, a layer of cheese, a layer of sauce, then another layer of tortillas.

4. Layer again with squash, cheese and sauce. Finish with a layer of tortillas, sauce and the remaining cheese. Cover and cook on low for 2 hours, until the tortillas are soft and the cheese is melted and bubbling. Serve immediately.

PEPPERS STUFFED WITH FARRO, FETA & HERBS

SERVES: *4* | **PREP:** *20 mins* | **COOK:** *3–4 hours*

INGREDIENTS

4 large red peppers
200 g/7 oz farro, cooked
2 garlic cloves, crushed
100 g/3½ oz black olives, stoned
*   and halved*
5 spring onions, finely sliced
100 g/3½ oz vegetarian feta cheese,
*   crumbled*
2 tbsp chopped fresh basil
2 tbsp chopped fresh parsley
2 tbsp olive oil
salt and pepper (optional)

1. Slice the tops off the red peppers just below the stems, remove the seeds and slice a very thin layer from the base of each pepper so they will sit flat in the slow cooker.

2. Put the farro, garlic, olives, spring onions, cheese, herbs and oil in a large mixing bowl and combine well. Season with salt and pepper, if using.

3. Stuff the mixture into the peppers, add the pepper tops, then place them in the base of the slow cooker. Cover and cook on high for 3–4 hours until the peppers are tender. Serve immediately.

LOUISIANA COURGETTES

SERVES: *6* | **PREP:** *20 mins* | **COOK:** *2 hours 30 mins*

INGREDIENTS

1 kg/2 lb 4 oz courgettes, thickly
*   sliced*
1 onion, finely chopped
2 garlic cloves, finely chopped
2 red peppers, deseeded and
*   chopped*
5 tbsp hot vegetable stock
4 tomatoes, peeled and chopped
25 g/1 oz butter, diced
salt and cayenne pepper (optional)
crusty bread, to serve

1. Place the courgettes, onion, garlic and red peppers in the slow cooker and season to taste with salt and cayenne pepper, if using. Pour in the stock and mix well.

2. Sprinkle the chopped tomatoes on top and dot with the butter. Cover and cook on high for 2½ hours until tender.

3. Serve immediately with crusty bread.

VEGETABLE CURRY

SERVES: *4–6* | **PREP:** *25 mins* | **COOK:** *5 hours 25 mins*

INGREDIENTS

2 tbsp vegetable oil

1 tsp cumin seeds

1 onion, sliced

2 curry leaves

2.5-cm/1-inch piece fresh ginger,
*   finely chopped*

2 fresh red chillies, deseeded and
*   chopped*

2 tbsp vegetarian Indian curry
*   paste*

2 carrots, sliced

115 g/4 oz mangetout

1 cauliflower, cut into florets

3 tomatoes, peeled and chopped

85 g/3 oz frozen peas

½ tsp ground turmeric

150–225 ml/5–8 fl oz vegetable
*   stock*

1. Heat the oil in a large, heavy-based saucepan. Add the cumin seeds and cook, stirring constantly, for 1–2 minutes until they give off their aroma and begin to pop. Add the onion and curry leaves and cook, stirring occasionally, for 5 minutes until the onion is soft. Add the ginger and chillies and cook, stirring occasionally, for 1 minute.

2. Stir in the curry paste and cook, stirring, for 2 minutes, then add the carrots, mangetout and cauliflower. Cook for 5 minutes, then add the tomatoes, peas and turmeric. Cook for a further 3 minutes, then add 150 ml/5 fl oz of the stock and bring to the boil.

3. Transfer the mixture to the slow cooker. If the vegetables are not covered by the liquid, add more hot stock, then cover and cook on low for 5 hours until tender. Remove and discard the curry leaves. Transfer to warmed serving dishes and serve immediately.

BAKED AUBERGINE WITH COURGETTE & TOMATO

SERVES: *4* | **PREP:** *20–25 mins* | **COOK:** *4 hours 20 mins*

INGREDIENTS

2 large aubergines

1 tbsp olive oil, for brushing

2 large courgettes, sliced

4 tomatoes, sliced

1 garlic clove, finely chopped

15 g/½ oz dry breadcrumbs

15 g/½ oz freshly grated Parmesan-style vegetarian cheese

salt and pepper (optional)

fresh basil leaves, torn, to garnish

1. Cut the aubergines into fairly thin slices and brush with oil. Heat a large griddle pan or heavy-based frying pan over a high heat, then add the aubergines and cook in batches for 6–8 minutes, turning once, until soft and brown.

2. Layer the aubergines in the slow cooker with the courgettes, tomatoes and garlic, seasoning to taste with salt and pepper, if using, between the layers.

3. Mix the breadcrumbs with the cheese and sprinkle over the vegetables. Cover and cook on low for 4 hours. Serve immediately, garnished with basil.

TOFU WITH SPICY PEANUT SAUCE

SERVES: *4* | **PREP:** *20 mins* | **COOK:** *4 hours 15 mins*

INGREDIENTS

675 g/1 lb 8 oz extra-firm tofu
2 tbsp vegetable oil
85 g/3 oz smooth peanut butter
3 tbsp low-sodium soy sauce
3 tbsp unseasoned rice vinegar
juice of 1 lime
2 tbsp soft light brown sugar
2 tsp toasted sesame oil
2 garlic cloves, finely chopped
1 tbsp finely chopped fresh ginger
2 jalapeño chillies, deseeded and
  finely chopped
350 g/12 oz baby spinach leaves
chopped fresh coriander, to serve
steamed rice, to serve

1. Slice the tofu into 2.5-cm/1-inch thick slabs and pat very dry with kitchen paper, pressing to release any excess moisture. Cut into 2.5-cm/1-inch cubes.

2. Heat the vegetable oil in a large, non-stick frying pan over a medium–high heat. Add the tofu, in batches, if necessary, and cook on one side for about 3 minutes until brown. Turn and cook on the other side for a further 3 minutes until brown.

3. Meanwhile, put the peanut butter, soy sauce, vinegar, lime juice, sugar, sesame oil, garlic, ginger and chillies into the slow cooker and mix to combine.

4. Add the tofu to the slow cooker. Stir gently to coat, cover and cook on low for about 4 hours.

5. About 15 minutes before serving, place the spinach in the slow cooker on top of the cooked tofu mixture, re-cover and cook for about 15 minutes, until the spinach is wilted. Stir in the coriander and serve immediately with steamed rice.

VEGETARIAN
PAELLA

SERVES: 6 | **PREP:** 25 mins | **COOK:** 2 hours 45 mins–3 hours 15 mins

INGREDIENTS

4 tbsp olive oil
1 Spanish onion, sliced
2 garlic cloves, finely chopped
1 litre/1¾ pints hot vegetable stock
large pinch of saffron threads,
  lightly crushed
1 yellow pepper, deseeded and
  sliced
1 red pepper, deseeded and sliced
1 large aubergine, diced
225 g/8 oz paella or risotto rice
450 g/1 lb tomatoes, peeled and
  chopped
115 g/4 oz chestnut mushrooms,
  sliced
115 g/4 oz French beans, halved
400 g/14 oz canned borlotti beans,
  drained and rinsed
salt and pepper (optional)

1. Heat the oil in a large frying pan. Add the onion and garlic and cook over a low heat, stirring occasionally, for 5 minutes until soft. Put 3 tablespoons of the stock into a small bowl and stir in the saffron, then set aside to infuse.

2. Add the yellow and red peppers and aubergine to the pan and cook, stirring occasionally, for 5 minutes. Add the rice and cook, stirring constantly, for 1 minute until the grains are coated with oil and glistening. Pour in the remaining stock and add the tomatoes, mushrooms, French beans and borlotti beans. Stir in the saffron mixture and season to taste with salt and pepper, if using.

3. Transfer the mixture to the slow cooker, cover and cook on low for 2½–3 hours, until the rice is tender and the stock has been absorbed. Transfer to warmed serving plates and serve immediately.

CHAPTER TWO

POULTRY

SPRING CHICKEN STEW
WITH CHIVE DUMPLINGS

SERVES: *5* | **PREP:** *30 mins* | **COOK:** *4 hours*

INGREDIENTS

1 large onion, finely chopped
3 celery sticks, diced
2 garlic cloves, diced
3 leeks, chopped into thin rounds
8 skinless, boneless chicken thighs
70 g/2½ oz pearl barley
small bunch of fresh thyme
juice and zest of 1 lemon
500 ml/18 fl oz chicken stock
100 g/3½ oz frozen peas
1 small courgette, cut into thin
  crescents
50 g/1¾ oz baby spinach
salt and pepper (optional)

DUMPLINGS

50 g/1¾ oz butter, softened
125 g/4½ oz self-raising flour
40 g/1½ oz Cheddar cheese,
  crumbled
1 tbsp snipped fresh chives
3–4 tbsp cold water

1. Place the onion, celery, garlic, leeks, chicken, barley, thyme and lemon zest and juice in the slow cooker. Pour over the stock and season with salt and pepper, if using. Cover and cook on high for 3 hours.

2. Meanwhile, make the dumplings. Rub the butter into the flour and mix in the cheese and chives. Add just enough cold water to bring the mixture together to form a soft dough and divide the dough into 5–6 small dumplings.

3. Stir the peas, courgette and spinach into the stew. Add the dumplings, re-cover and cook on high for a further 1 hour. Serve, sprinkled with pepper, if using.

MEXICAN CHICKEN BOWLS

SERVES: *4* | **PREP:** *10 mins* | **COOK:** *4–5 hours*

INGREDIENTS

*8 boneless chicken thighs, skin
  removed, trimmed of fat*
6 large shallots, quartered
4 garlic cloves, peeled
400 g/14 oz canned black beans
*200 g/7 oz canned sweetcorn,
  drained (150 g/5½ oz drained
  weight)*
200 g/7 oz brown rice
½ tsp cayenne pepper
1 green pepper, deseeded and sliced
1 green chilli, sliced
juice of 1 lime
300 ml/10 fl oz vegetable stock
150 ml/5 fl oz boiling water
salt and pepper (optional)
2 small avocados, sliced, to garnish
*2 tbsp roughly chopped fresh
  coriander, to garnish*
*100 ml/3½ fl oz soured cream,
  to serve*

1. Place the chicken, shallots, garlic, beans, sweetcorn, rice, cayenne pepper, green pepper and chilli in the slow cooker. Squeeze over the lime juice and pour over the stock. Season with salt and pepper, if using. Cover and cook on high for 4–5 hours until the rice is soft.

2. Stir through the boiling water to loosen the stew.

3. Transfer to warmed bowls, garnish with avocado and coriander and serve with soured cream.

COCK-A-LEEKIE SOUP

SERVES: *6–8* | **PREP:** *10 mins* | **COOK:** *7 hours 30 mins*

INGREDIENTS

12 prunes, stoned, or 12 ready-to-
*   eat prunes*
4 chicken portions
450 g/1 lb leeks, sliced
1.4 litres/2½ pints hot chicken stock
*   or hot beef stock*
1 bouquet garni
salt and pepper (optional)

1. If using ordinary prunes, place them in a bowl and add cold water to cover. Set aside to soak while the soup is cooking.

2. Place the chicken portions and leeks in the slow cooker. Pour in the stock, add the bouquet garni, cover and cook on low for 7 hours.

3. If you are going to serve the chicken in the soup, remove it from the cooker with a slotted spoon and cut the meat off the bones. Cut the meat into bite-sized pieces and return it to the cooker. Otherwise, leave the chicken portions in the slow cooker.

4. Drain the prunes, if necessary. Add the prunes to the soup and season to taste with salt and pepper, if using. Re-cover and cook on high for 30 minutes.

5. Remove and discard the bouquet garni. Ladle the soup into warmed bowls and serve immediately.

CHICKEN NOODLE SOUP

SERVES: *4* | **PREP:** *25 mins* | **COOK:** *5 hours 35 mins*

INGREDIENTS

1 onion, diced

2 celery sticks, diced

2 carrots, diced

1 kg/2 lb 4 oz oven-ready chicken

700 ml/1¼ pints hot chicken stock

1 tsp salt

115 g/4 oz dried egg tagliatelle

salt and pepper (optional)

*2 tbsp chopped fresh dill, plus extra
   to garnish*

1. Place the onion, celery and carrots in the slow cooker. Season the chicken all over with salt and pepper, if using, and place on top. Pour the stock over. Cover and cook on low for 5 hours.

2. Leaving the juices in the slow cooker, carefully lift out the chicken and remove the meat from the carcass, discarding the bones and skin. Cut the meat into bite-sized pieces.

3. Skim the excess fat from the juices, then return the chicken to the slow cooker and increase the heat to high.

4. Add 1 teaspoon of salt to a large saucepan of water and bring to the boil. Add the pasta, bring back to the boil and cook for 8–10 minutes, or until tender but still firm to the bite. Drain, add to the slow cooker and stir well.

5. Add the dill to the soup and stir well. Cover and cook on high for a further 20 minutes. Garnish with extra dill and serve immediately.

CHICKEN & MUSHROOM STEW

SERVES: *4* | **PREP:** *20 mins* | **COOK:** *7 hours 35 mins*

INGREDIENTS

15 g/½ oz unsalted butter

2 tbsp olive oil

1.8 kg/4 lb skinless chicken portions

2 red onions, sliced

2 garlic cloves, finely chopped

400 g/14 oz canned chopped tomatoes

2 tbsp chopped fresh flat-leaf parsley

6 fresh basil leaves, torn

1 tbsp sun-dried tomato purée

150 ml/5 fl oz red wine

225 g/8 oz mushrooms, sliced

salt and pepper (optional)

1. Heat the butter and oil in a heavy-based frying pan. Add the chicken, in batches if necessary, and cook over a medium–high heat, turning frequently, for 10 minutes until golden brown all over. Using a slotted spoon, transfer the chicken to the slow cooker.

2. Add the onions and garlic to the pan and cook over a low heat, stirring occasionally, for 10 minutes until golden. Add the tomatoes with their can juices, stir in the parsley, basil, tomato purée and wine and season to taste with salt and pepper, if using. Bring to the boil, then pour the mixture over the chicken.

3. Cover the slow cooker and cook on low for 6½ hours. Stir in the mushrooms, re-cover and cook on high for 30 minutes, until the chicken is tender and the vegetables are cooked through. Taste and adjust the seasoning if necessary and serve immediately.

SLOW ROAST
CHICKEN

SERVES: *4–6* | **PREP:** *15 mins* | **COOK:** *7 hours*

INGREDIENTS

1.5-kg/3 lb 5-oz oven-ready chicken
½ lemon
1 tbsp olive oil
½ tsp dried thyme
½ tsp paprika
salt and pepper (optional)

1. Wipe the chicken with kitchen paper and tuck the lemon inside the body cavity. Brush the oil over the chicken skin and sprinkle with thyme, paprika, and salt and pepper, if using, rubbing in with your fingers to cover all the skin.

2. Place the chicken in the slow cooker, cover and cook on high for 3 hours. Reduce the heat to low and cook for a further 4 hours, until the chicken is tender and cooked through and the juices run clear when a skewer is inserted into the thickest part of the meat.

3. Carefully remove the chicken from the slow cooker and place on a warmed platter. Skim any fat from the juices and spoon the juices over the chicken. Serve immediately.

NUTTY CHICKEN

SERVES: *4* | **PREP:** *15 mins* | **COOK:** *6 hours 25 mins*

INGREDIENTS

3 tbsp sunflower oil

4 skinless chicken portions

2 shallots, chopped

1 tsp ground ginger

1 tbsp plain flour

425 ml/15 fl oz beef stock

55 g/2 oz walnut pieces

grated rind of 1 lemon

2 tbsp lemon juice

1 tbsp black treacle

salt and pepper (optional)

4 pea shoots, to garnish

1. Heat the oil in a large, heavy-based frying pan. Season the chicken portions with salt and pepper, if using, and add to the pan. Cook over a medium heat, turning occasionally, for 5–8 minutes until light golden all over. Transfer to the slow cooker.

2. Add the shallots to the pan and cook, stirring occasionally, for 3–4 minutes until soft. Sprinkle in the ginger and flour and cook, stirring constantly, for 1 minute. Gradually stir in the stock and bring to the boil, stirring constantly. Reduce the heat and simmer for 1 minute, then stir in the walnuts, lemon rind, lemon juice and treacle.

3. Pour the sauce over the chicken. Cover and cook on low for 6 hours, until the chicken is cooked through and tender. Taste and adjust the seasoning, if using. Transfer the chicken to warmed plates and spoon some of the sauce over each portion. Garnish with pea shoots and serve immediately.

CHICKEN QUESADILLAS

SERVES: *4* | **PREP:** *25 mins, plus marinating* | **COOK:** *2 hours 10 mins*

INGREDIENTS

4 skinless, boneless chicken breasts

½ tsp crushed dried chillies

2 garlic cloves, crushed

2 tbsp chopped fresh parsley

2 tbsp olive oil

350 g/12 oz cherry tomatoes

4 large wheat tortillas

250 g/9 oz mozzarella cheese

salt and pepper (optional)

1. Place the chicken in a bowl with the chillies, garlic, parsley and 1 tablespoon of the olive oil, and turn to coat evenly. Cover and leave in the refrigerator to marinate for at least 1 hour, or overnight.

2. Tip the tomatoes into the slow cooker and arrange the chicken breasts on top. Season to taste with salt and pepper, if using. Cover and cook on high for 2 hours, or until tender.

3. Remove the chicken and shred the meat using two forks. Place on one side of each tortilla and top with the tomatoes. Chop or tear the cheese and arrange on top. Moisten the edges of the tortillas and fold over to enclose the filling.

4. Brush a griddle pan or large frying pan with the remaining oil and place over a medium heat. Add the quesadillas to the pan and cook until golden, turning once. Cut into wedges and serve immediately with any remaining juices spooned over.

EASY CHINESE CHICKEN

SERVES: *4* | **PREP:** *15 mins* | **COOK:** *4 hours 10 mins*

INGREDIENTS

2 tsp freshly grated ginger

4 garlic cloves, finely chopped

2 star anise

*150 ml/5 fl oz Chinese rice wine or
   medium-dry sherry*

2 tbsp dark soy sauce

1 tsp sesame oil

5 tbsp water

*4 skinless chicken thighs or
   drumsticks*

cooked rice, to serve

1. Mix the ginger, garlic, star anise, rice wine, soy sauce, sesame oil and water together in a bowl. Place the chicken in a saucepan, add the spice mixture and bring to the boil.

2. Transfer to the slow cooker, cover and cook on low for 4 hours, or until the chicken is tender and cooked through.

3. Remove and discard the star anise. Transfer the chicken to warmed serving plates, garnish with shredded spring onions and serve immediately with rice.

CHICKEN CACCIATORE

SERVES: *4* | **PREP:** *15 mins* | **COOK:** *5 hours 25 mins*

INGREDIENTS

3 tbsp olive oil

4 skinless chicken portions

2 onions, sliced

2 garlic cloves, finely chopped

400 g/14 oz canned chopped
tomatoes

1 tbsp tomato purée

2 tbsp chopped fresh parsley

2 tsp fresh thyme leaves, plus extra
sprigs to garnish

150 ml/5 fl oz red wine

salt and pepper (optional)

1. Heat the oil in a heavy-based frying pan. Add the chicken and cook over a medium heat, turning occasionally, for 10 minutes, until golden all over. Using a slotted spoon, transfer the chicken to the slow cooker.

2. Add the onions to the pan and cook, stirring occasionally, for 5 minutes until soft and just turning golden. Add the garlic, tomatoes, tomato purée, parsley, thyme leaves and wine. Season to taste with salt and pepper, if using, and bring to the boil.

3. Pour the tomato mixture over the chicken pieces. Cover and cook on low for 5 hours until the chicken is tender and cooked through. Taste and adjust the seasoning, if using. Transfer to warmed serving plates, garnish with thyme sprigs and serve immediately.

PARMESAN CHICKEN

SERVES: *4* | **PREP:** *20 mins* | **COOK:** *4 hours 25 mins*

INGREDIENTS

1 egg, beaten

4 skinless, boneless chicken breasts

85 g/3 oz fine dry breadcrumbs

2 tbsp olive oil

350 g/12 oz ready-made tomato-based pasta sauce

4 thin slices Cheddar cheese

115 g/4 oz finely grated Parmesan cheese

salt and pepper (optional)

1. Season the egg with salt and pepper, if using. Dip each chicken breast in the egg, turning to coat evenly, then dip into the breadcrumbs, lightly pressing down to cover evenly.

2. Heat the oil in a frying pan over a high heat, add the chicken breasts and fry for 3–4 minutes until golden brown, turning once.

3. Pour the pasta sauce into the slow cooker and place the chicken breasts on top in a single layer. Cover and cook on low for 4 hours.

4. Place a slice of Cheddar cheese on top of each chicken breast and sprinkle with Parmesan cheese. Re-cover and cook on high for a further 20 minutes. Serve immediately.

CHIPOTLE CHICKEN

SERVES: *4* | **PREP:** *15 mins, plus soaking* | **COOK:** *5 hours 10 mins*

INGREDIENTS

4–6 dried chipotle chillies

4 garlic cloves, unpeeled

1 small onion, chopped

400 g/14 oz canned chopped tomatoes

300 ml/10 fl oz hot chicken stock or hot vegetable stock

4 skinless chicken breasts

salt and pepper (optional)

4 tsp chopped fresh coriander, to garnish

1. Preheat the oven to 200°C/400°F/Gas Mark 6. Place the chillies in a bowl and pour in just enough hot water to cover. Set aside to soak for 30 minutes. Meanwhile, place the garlic cloves on a baking sheet and roast in the preheated oven for about 10 minutes until soft. Remove from the oven and set aside to cool.

2. Drain the chillies, reserving 125 ml/4 fl oz of the soaking water. Deseed the chillies, if liked, and roughly chop. Place the chillies and reserved soaking water in a blender or food processor and process to a purée. Peel the garlic and mash in a bowl.

3. Place the chilli purée, garlic, onion and tomatoes in the slow cooker and stir in the stock. Season the chicken with salt and pepper to taste, if using, and place in the slow cooker. Cover and cook on low for about 5 hours until the chicken is tender and cooked through.

4. Lift the chicken out of the slow cooker with a slotted spoon, cover and keep warm. Pour the cooking liquid into a saucepan and bring to the boil on the hob. Boil for 5–10 minutes until reduced. Transfer the chicken to warmed serving plates and pour the sauce over the chicken. Serve immediately garnished with coriander.

CHICKEN PARMIGIANA

SERVES: *4* | **PREP:** *15 mins* | **COOK:** *8 hours 25 mins–9 hours 25 mins*

INGREDIENTS

4 chicken portions, about 250 g/
9 oz each
100 ml/3½ fl oz olive oil
3 red onions, thinly sliced
2 garlic cloves, finely chopped
1 red pepper, deseeded and thinly
sliced
115 g/4 oz mushrooms, sliced
2 tsp chopped fresh thyme
1 tbsp chopped fresh flat-leaf
parsley
400 g/14 oz canned chopped
tomatoes
4 tbsp dry white vermouth
425 ml/15 fl oz chicken stock
85 g/3 oz freshly grated Parmesan
cheese
salt and pepper (optional)
cooked pappardelle, to serve

1. Season the chicken with salt and pepper to taste, if using. Heat the oil in a large, heavy-based saucepan. Add the chicken and cook over a medium heat for 5–6 minutes on each side until brown all over. Using tongs, transfer the chicken to the slow cooker.

2. Add the onions, garlic, red pepper, mushrooms, thyme, parsley, tomatoes, vermouth and stock to the pan. Season to taste with salt and pepper, if using, and bring to the boil, stirring occasionally. Transfer the mixture to the slow cooker, cover and cook on low for 8–9 hours until the chicken is cooked through and tender.

3. Transfer to warmed plates and sprinkle over the cheese. Serve immediately with pappardelle.

CHICKEN BREASTS STUFFED WITH HERBED GOAT'S CHEESE

SERVES: *4* | **PREP:** *25 mins* | **COOK:** *2 hours 10 mins–4 hours 10 mins*

INGREDIENTS

225 g/8 oz soft, fresh goat's cheese

10 g/¼ oz fresh basil leaves, finely chopped

2 spring onions, thinly sliced

2 garlic cloves, finely chopped

4 boneless, skinless chicken breasts

2 tbsp olive oil

200 g/7 oz chard, central ribs removed, cut into wide ribbons

225 ml/8 fl oz dry white wine, chicken stock or water

salt and pepper (optional)

1. Put the cheese, basil, spring onions and garlic into a mixing bowl and stir to combine.

2. Lay the chicken breasts flat on a chopping board. Working with one breast at a time, place your hand on top of the breast and press down to keep it in place. With the other hand, use a large, sharp knife to slice the breast horizontally, leaving one edge intact like a hinge.

3. Open the butterflied breasts and spoon equal amounts of the cheese mixture onto one half of each. Fold closed and secure with wooden cocktail sticks or kitchen string. Season to taste with salt and pepper, if using.

4. Heat the oil in a large frying pan over a medium–high heat until very hot, then add the chicken. Cook on one side for 4 minutes until brown, then turn and cook on the other side for a further 4 minutes until brown.

5. Put the chard and the wine into the slow cooker. Arrange the stuffed chicken breasts on top of the chard, cover and cook on high for about 2 hours or on low for about 4 hours until the chicken is cooked through. Serve immediately.

BULGARIAN CHICKEN

SERVES: *6* | **PREP:** *15 mins* | **COOK:** *6 hours 15 mins*

INGREDIENTS

2 tbsp sunflower oil

6 chicken portions

2 onions, chopped

2 garlic cloves, finely chopped

1 fresh red chilli, deseeded and
  finely chopped

6 tomatoes, peeled and chopped

2 tsp sweet paprika

1 bay leaf

225 ml/8 fl oz chicken stock

salt and pepper (optional)

1. Heat the oil in a large, heavy-based frying pan. Add the chicken portions and cook over a medium heat, turning occasionally, for about 10 minutes until brown all over.

2. Transfer the chicken to the slow cooker and add the onions, garlic, chilli and tomatoes. Sprinkle in the paprika, add the bay leaf and pour in the stock. Season to taste with salt and pepper, if using. Stir well, cover and cook on low for 6 hours until the chicken is cooked through and tender.

3. Remove and discard the bay leaf. Transfer to warmed serving plates and serve immediately.

TURKEY CHILLI WITH SWEET POTATOES

INGREDIENTS

1 tbsp vegetable oil

1 onion, diced

675 g/1 lb 8 oz fresh turkey mince

70 g/2½ oz tomato purée

1 tbsp mild chilli powder

1 tsp ground cumin

*2 canned chipotle chillies in adobo
    sauce, deseeded and diced, plus 2
    teaspoons of the adobo sauce (or
    substitute 1 tsp ground chipotles)*

1 tsp salt

*400 g/14 oz canned chopped
    tomatoes*

450 ml/16 fl oz chicken stock

*1 large sweet potato (about 225 g/
    8 oz), diced*

TO SERVE

fresh coriander

soured cream

grated Cheddar cheese

diced avocado

finely chopped red onion

1. Heat the oil in a large frying pan. Add the onion and cook, stirring, for about 5 minutes until soft. Add the turkey and cook, breaking up the meat with a wooden spoon, for about 4 minutes until brown all over. Stir in the tomato purée, chilli powder, cumin, chillies, adobo sauce and salt and cook for a further 1 minute.

2. Transfer the mixture to the slow cooker. Stir in the tomatoes, stock and sweet potato. Cover and cook on high for 4 hours or on low for 8 hours. Serve immediately, accompanied by coriander, soured cream, cheese, avocado and red onion.

TURKEY & RICE CASSEROLE

SERVES: 4 | **PREP:** 20 mins | **COOK:** 2 hours 5 mins

INGREDIENTS

1 tbsp olive oil

500 g/1 lb 2 oz diced turkey breast

1 onion, diced

2 carrots, diced

2 celery sticks, sliced

250 g/9 oz closed-cup mushrooms,
* sliced*

175 g/6 oz long-grain rice,
* preferably basmati*

450 ml/16 fl oz hot chicken stock

salt and pepper (optional)

1. Heat the oil in a heavy-based frying pan, add the turkey and fry over a high heat for 3–4 minutes until light brown all over.

2. Combine the onion, carrots, celery, mushrooms and rice in the slow cooker. Arrange the turkey on top, season well with salt and pepper, if using, and pour the stock over. Cover and cook on high for 2 hours.

3. Stir with a fork to mix and serve immediately in warmed bowls.

TURKEY MEATLOAF

SERVES: *4* | **PREP:** *20 mins* | **COOK:** *4 hours*

INGREDIENTS

vegetable oil, for oiling

600 g/1 lb 5 oz fresh turkey mince

1 onion, finely chopped

55 g/2 oz porridge oats

2 tbsp chopped fresh sage

2 tbsp Worcestershire sauce

1 egg, beaten

salt and pepper (optional)

1. Place a trivet in the base of the slow cooker. Grease and line a 900-g/2-lb loaf tin, or a loaf tin that fits into your slow cooker.

2. Mix the remaining ingredients together and season to taste with salt and pepper, if using.

3. Spoon the mixture into the prepared tin and smooth the top level with a palette knife.

4. Place the loaf in the slow cooker and place a piece of greaseproof paper on top. Cover and cook on low for 4 hours, until firm and the juices run clear, not pink, when the loaf is pierced with a skewer.

5. Turn out the loaf and serve sliced.

TURKEY BREAST WITH BACON, LEEKS & PRUNES

SERVES: *6–8* | **PREP:** *25 mins* | **COOK:** *5 hours 20 mins–9 hours 20 mins, plus resting*

INGREDIENTS

115 g/4 oz bacon rashers

2 leeks, trimmed, white and light green parts thinly sliced

1 skinless, bone-in turkey breast (about 1.8 kg/4 lb)

25 g/1 oz plain flour

1 tbsp olive oil, if needed

12 stoned prunes, halved (quartered, if large)

1 tsp crumbled dried thyme or 1 tbsp finely chopped fresh thyme

225 ml/8 fl oz chicken stock

salt and pepper (optional)

1. Heat a frying pan over a medium–high heat, then add the bacon and cook until just crisp. Remove from the pan, drain on kitchen paper, then chop or crumble into small pieces.

2. Add the leeks to the pan and cook in the remaining fat over a medium–high heat, stirring frequently, for about 5 minutes until soft.

3. Season the turkey well with salt and pepper, if using, and dredge with the flour. If needed, add the oil to the pan, then add the turkey and cook on one side for 4–5 minutes until brown. Turn and cook on the other side for a further 4–5 minutes until brown.

4. Place the turkey in the slow cooker together with the leeks, bacon, prunes and thyme. Add the stock, cover and cook on high for about 5 hours or on low for about 9 hours.

5. Remove the turkey from the slow cooker and leave to rest for 5 minutes. Slice and serve with some of the sauce, including the prunes and bits of bacon, spooned over the top.

TURKEY HASH

INGREDIENTS

1 tbsp olive oil

500 g/1 lb 2 oz fresh turkey mince

1 large red onion, diced

550 g/1 lb 4 oz butternut squash,
   diced

2 celery sticks, sliced

500 g/1 lb 2 oz potatoes, peeled and
   diced

3 tbsp Worcestershire sauce

2 bay leaves

salt and pepper (optional)

1. Heat the oil in a frying pan, add the turkey and fry over a high heat, stirring, until broken up and light brown all over.

2. Place all the vegetables in the slow cooker, then add the turkey and the pan juices. Add the Worcestershire sauce and bay leaves and season to taste with salt and pepper, if using. Cover and cook on low for 7 hours. Serve immediately.

CHAPTER THREE

MEAT

• • •

KALE, QUINOA & CAULIFLOWER SOUP

SERVES: *4* | **PREP:** *20 mins* | **COOK:** *4 hours 10 mins*

INGREDIENTS

2 tbsp olive oil

2 small onions, finely diced

4 garlic cloves, sliced

1 tsp smoked paprika

100 g/3½ oz quinoa

2 litres/3½ pints hot vegetable stock or chicken stock

1 small head of cauliflower, about 250 g/9 oz, broken into very small florets

200 g/7 oz curly kale, washed and finely chopped

juice and zest of 1 lemon

100 g/3½ oz chorizo, sliced

salt and pepper (optional)

2 tbsp fresh flat-leaf parsley, roughly chopped, to garnish

pinch of smoked paprika, to garnish

4 tbsp natural yogurt, to serve

1. Heat the oil in a large frying pan. Add the onion and garlic and cook over a medium heat for 3–4 minutes until soft. Sprinkle over the smoked paprika and cook for a further 1 minute.

2. Add the onion and garlic to the slow cooker with the quinoa, stock and cauliflower. Cover and cook on high for 3 hours.

3. Stir in the kale, re-cover and cook for a further 1 hour. Season with salt and pepper, if using, and stir through the lemon zest and juice.

4. While the soup is cooking, heat a small frying pan over a medium heat. Add the chorizo and fry until crispy.

5. To serve, ladle the soup into warmed bowls, add the chorizo, garnish with parsley and paprika and add a tablespoon of yogurt to each bowl.

BOSTON BAKED BEANS

SERVES: *4* | **PREP:** *20 mins* | **COOK:** *8 hours 15 mins*

INGREDIENTS

350 g/12 oz dried cannellini beans,
* soaked in cold water overnight,*
* or for at least 5 hours*
1 large onion, cut in half
2 bay leaves
100 ml/3½ fl oz maple syrup
70 g/2½ oz soft light brown sugar
1 tbsp black treacle
1 tsp chilli flakes
1 tbsp Worcestershire sauce
1 tbsp Dijon mustard
200 g/7 oz bacon lardons or pork
* belly, cut into 2-cm/¾-inch pieces*
150 ml/5 fl oz water

1. Drain and rinse the beans, place in a saucepan, cover with fresh cold water and bring to the boil. Boil rapidly for at least 10 minutes, then remove from the heat, drain the beans and rinse again.

2. Put the beans in the slow cooker with the onion, bay leaves, syrup, sugar, treacle, chilli, Worcestershire sauce and mustard.

3. Stir the lardons into the mixture and add the water.

4. Cover and cook on low for 8 hours, until the beans are tender and the sauce is syrupy. If you can, stir the contents halfway through the cooking time. Remove the bay leaves, transfer to warmed bowls and serve immediately.

HAM COOKED
IN CIDER

SERVES: *6* | **PREP:** *20 mins* | **COOK:** *8 hours, plus standing*

INGREDIENTS

*1 kg/2 lb 4 oz boneless gammon
  joint*

1 onion, halved

4 cloves

6 black peppercorns

1 tsp juniper berries

1 celery stick, chopped

1 carrot, sliced

1 litre/1¾ pints medium cider

fresh salad, to serve

1. Place a trivet or rack in the slow cooker, if you like, and stand the gammon on it. Otherwise, just place the gammon in the slow cooker. Stud each onion half with two of the cloves and add to the slow cooker with the peppercorns, juniper berries, celery and carrot.

2. Pour in the cider, cover and cook on low for 8 hours, until the meat is tender.

3. Remove the gammon from the cooker and place on a board. Tent with foil and leave to stand for 10–15 minutes. Discard the cooking liquid and flavourings.

4. Cut any rind and fat off the gammon joint and carve into slices. Transfer to serving plates and serve immediately with a fresh salad.

PORK STUFFED WITH APPLES

SERVES: *4* | **PREP:** *25 mins* | **COOK:** *4–7 hours*

INGREDIENTS

1 large apple, peeled, cored and
sliced
125 ml/4 fl oz apple juice or water
4 boneless pork chops, about
2.5 cm/1 inch thick
4 slices prosciutto
115 g/4 oz Gorgonzola cheese
salt and pepper (optional)
mashed potato, to serve

1. Place half of the apple slices in the base of the slow cooker and add the apple juice.

2. Butterfly the pork chops by laying each chop flat on a chopping board, then, pressing down on it with the flat of your hand to keep it in place, cut through the centre horizontally, leaving one side attached like a hinge. Loosely wrap in clingfilm and gently pound with a meat mallet to a thickness of about 2 cm/¾ inch.

3. Open the flattened and butterflied chops like books and place on the chopping board. Layer each chop with a slice of prosciutto, a quarter of the cheese and a quarter of the remaining apple slices. Fold closed and secure with wooden cocktail sticks.

4. Season the stuffed chops all over with salt and pepper, if using, and place in the slow cooker on top of the apple slices. Cover and cook on high for about 4 hours or on low for about 7 hours until the meat is cooked through. Serve immediately with mashed potato.

HUNGARIAN PORK GOULASH

SERVES: *4* | **PREP:** *20 mins* | **COOK:** *8 hours 10 mins*

INGREDIENTS

2 tsp olive oil

*2 kg/4 lb 8 oz off-the-bone pork
    shoulder joint, skin removed, fat
    left on*

2 red onions, finely sliced

3 garlic cloves, sliced

1 tbsp smoked mild paprika

2 tsp caraway seeds

*1 small bunch of fresh oregano,
    leaves picked*

4 peppers, mixed colours

400 g/14 oz canned plum tomatoes

100 ml/3½ fl oz vegetable stock

4 tbsp red wine vinegar

salt and pepper (optional)

*pinch of smoked mild paprika and
    2 tbsp chopped fresh parsley, to
    garnish*

*soured cream and cooked rice,
    to serve*

1. Heat the oil in a large frying pan over a high heat. Using tongs, sear the pork shoulder for 6–8 minutes until the meat takes on some colour and the fat renders down.

2. Add the onions, garlic, paprika and caraway seeds to the slow cooker and place the pork shoulder joint on top. Nestle the oregano and whole peppers around the sides of the pork. Add the tomatoes, stock and vinegar. Season with salt and pepper, if using. Cover and cook on high for 8 hours, or until the pork is tender and falling apart.

3. Slice the pork and deseed and slice the peppers.

4. Transfer to warmed plates, garnish with paprika and parsley and serve with soured cream and rice.

SAUSAGE & BEAN CASSOULET

SERVES: *4* | **PREP:** *10–15 mins* | **COOK:** *6 hours 15 mins*

INGREDIENTS

2 tbsp sunflower oil

2 onions, chopped

2 garlic cloves, finely chopped

115 g/4 oz streaky bacon, chopped

500 g/1 lb 2 oz pork sausages

400 g/14 oz canned haricot, red kidney or black-eyed beans, drained and rinsed

2 tbsp chopped fresh parsley

150 ml/5 fl oz hot beef stock

4 slices French bread, to serve

55 g/2 oz Gruyère cheese, grated, to serve

1. Heat the oil in a heavy-based frying pan. Add the onions and cook over a low heat, stirring occasionally, for 5 minutes until soft. Add the garlic, bacon and sausages and cook, stirring and turning the sausages occasionally, for a further 5 minutes.

2. Using a slotted spoon, transfer the mixture from the pan to the slow cooker. Add the beans, parsley and stock, then cover and cook on low for 6 hours.

3. Shortly before serving, preheat the grill. Place the bread slices on the grill rack and lightly toast on one side under the preheated grill. Turn the slices over, sprinkle with the grated cheese and place under the grill until just melted.

4. Serve the cassoulet and the bread slices immediately.

SPICY PULLED PORK

SERVES: *4* | **PREP:** *25 mins* | **COOK:** *8 hours*

INGREDIENTS

2 onions, sliced

1.5 kg/3 lb 5 oz boned and rolled
*   pork shoulder*

2 tbsp demerara sugar

2 tbsp Worcestershire sauce

1 tbsp American mustard

2 tbsp tomato ketchup

1 tbsp cider vinegar

salt and pepper (optional)

burger buns or ciabatta rolls, to
*   serve*

1. Put the onions in the slow cooker and place the pork on top. Mix the sugar, Worcestershire sauce, mustard, ketchup and vinegar together and spread all over the surface of the pork. Season to taste with salt and pepper, if using. Cover and cook on low for 8 hours.

2. Remove the pork from the slow cooker and use two forks to pull it apart into shreds.

3. Skim any excess fat from the juices and stir a little juice into the pork. Serve the pork in burger buns, with the remaining juices for spooning over.

MEXICAN
PORK CHOPS

SERVES: *4* | **PREP:** *20 mins* | **COOK:** *6 hours 25 mins*

INGREDIENTS

4 pork chops, trimmed of excess fat

2 tbsp corn oil

*450 g/1 lb canned pineapple
    chunks in juice*

*1 red pepper, deseeded and finely
    chopped*

*2 fresh jalapeño chillies, deseeded
    and finely chopped*

1 onion, finely chopped

*1 tbsp chopped fresh coriander, plus
    extra sprigs to garnish*

125 ml/4 fl oz hot chicken stock

salt and pepper (optional)

flour tortillas, to serve

1. Season the chops with salt and pepper to taste, if using. Heat the oil in a large, heavy-based frying pan. Add the chops and cook over a medium heat for 2–3 minutes on each side until light brown in colour. Transfer them to the slow cooker. Drain the pineapple, reserving the juice, and set aside.

2. Add the red pepper, chillies and onion to the pan and cook, stirring occasionally, for 5 minutes until the onion is soft. Transfer the mixture to the slow cooker and add the chopped coriander, stock and 125 ml/4 fl oz of the reserved pineapple juice. Cover and cook on low for 6 hours until the chops are tender.

3. Add the pineapple chunks to the slow cooker, re-cover and cook on high for 15 minutes. Garnish with coriander sprigs and serve immediately with flour tortillas.

KOREAN BEEF STEW WITH KIMCHI & SESAME

SERVES: *4* | **PREP:** *15 mins* | **COOK:** *8 hours*

INGREDIENTS

900 g/2 lb chuck steak
500 g/1 lb 2 oz kimchi
1 large onion, sliced
1 tbsp grated fresh ginger
4 garlic cloves, crushed
1 bay leaf
¼ tsp pepper
2 tbsp rice wine
2 tbsp sesame oil
1 tbsp soy sauce
¼ tsp chilli powder
200 ml/7 fl oz water
salt (optional)
4 spring onions, chopped, to garnish
1 tbsp sesame seeds, to garnish
cooked black rice, to serve

1. Remove any obvious fat from the steak and cut it into 2–3-cm/¾–1¼-inch cubes. Place the steak, kimchi, onion, ginger, garlic, bay leaf, pepper, rice wine, oil, soy sauce and chilli powder in the slow cooker. Pour the water over and mix gently until combined. Season to taste with salt, if using.

2. Cover the slow cooker and cook on low for 8 hours, stirring every couple of hours if possible. Remove the bay leaf, transfer to warmed serving bowls, garnish with spring onions and sesame seeds and serve with black rice.

THAI BEEF CURRY

INGREDIENTS

75 g/2¾ oz Thai red curry paste

175 ml/6 fl oz unsweetened coconut milk

50 g/1¾ oz soft dark brown sugar

1 tbsp Thai fish sauce

75 g/2¾ oz smooth peanut butter

900 g/2 lb chuck steak, cut into 2.5-cm/1-inch dice

2 potatoes, diced

125 ml/4 fl oz beef stock or water

fresh basil leaves, cut into ribbons, to garnish

steamed rice, to serve

1. Put the curry paste, coconut milk, sugar, fish sauce and peanut butter into the slow cooker and stir to combine. Add the beef, potatoes and stock and stir to coat in the mixture.

2. Cover and cook on high for about 4 hours or on low for 8 hours, then set the lid slightly ajar and cook for a further 1 hour, or until the beef is very tender and the sauce has thickened slightly. Serve immediately, garnished with basil and accompanied with the steamed rice.

MOROCCAN SPICED BEEF STEW

SERVES: *4–6* | **PREP:** *20 mins* | **COOK:** *6 hours 10 mins–9 hours 10 mins*

INGREDIENTS

2 tbsp vegetable oil

1 onion, diced

1½ tsp salt

½ tsp pepper

2 tsp ground cumin

½ tsp ground cinnamon

½ tsp ground ginger

225 ml/8 fl oz red wine

675 g/1 lb 8 oz chuck steak, cut into
*   5-cm/2-inch pieces*

130 g/4¾ oz dried apricots, diced

2 tbsp clear honey

125 ml/4 fl oz water

chopped fresh coriander, to garnish

cooked couscous, to serve

1. Heat the oil in a large frying pan. Add the onion and cook, stirring, for about 5 minutes until soft. Add the salt, pepper, cumin, cinnamon and ginger and cook, stirring, for a further 1 minute.

2. Add the wine, bring to the boil and cook for 1 minute, scraping up any sediment from the base of the pan. Transfer the mixture to the slow cooker.

3. Add the beef, apricots, honey and water and stir. Cover and cook on high for 6 hours or on low for 9 hours until the meat is very tender.

4. Serve immediately with couscous, garnished with coriander.

BEEF
BOURGUIGNON

SERVES: 6 | **PREP:** 20 mins | **COOK:** 7 hours 30 mins

INGREDIENTS

2 tbsp plain flour

900 g/2 lb braising steak, trimmed
and cut into 2.5-cm/1-inch cubes

6 streaky bacon rashers, derinded
and chopped

3 tbsp olive oil

25 g/1 oz unsalted butter

12 baby onions or shallots

2 garlic cloves, finely chopped

150 ml/5 fl oz beef stock

450 ml/16 fl oz full-bodied red wine

1 bouquet garni

140 g/5 oz mushrooms, quartered

salt and pepper (optional)

1. Put the flour into a polythene food bag and season to taste with salt and pepper, if using. Add the steak cubes, in batches, hold the top securely and shake well to coat. Transfer the meat to a plate.

2. Add the bacon to a large, heavy-based saucepan and cook, stirring occasionally, until the fat runs and the bacon is crisp. Using a slotted spoon, transfer the bacon to a plate. Add the oil to the pan. When it is hot, add the steak and cook, in batches, stirring occasionally, for 5 minutes until brown all over. Transfer the steak to the plate with a slotted spoon.

3. Add the butter to the pan. When it has melted, add the onions and garlic and cook, stirring occasionally, for 5 minutes. Return the bacon and steak to the pan and pour in the stock and wine. Bring to the boil.

4. Transfer the mixture to the slow cooker and add the bouquet garni. Cover and cook on low for 7 hours until the meat is tender.

5. Add the mushrooms to the slow cooker and stir well. Re-cover and cook on high for 15 minutes.

6. Remove and discard the bouquet garni. Taste and adjust the seasoning, adding salt and pepper to taste, if using. Transfer to warmed serving bowls and serve immediately.

BEEF & CHIPOTLE
BURRITOS

SERVES: *4* | **PREP:** *25 mins* | **COOK:** *4 hours 10 mins*

INGREDIENTS

1 tbsp olive oil

1 onion, sliced

600 g/1 lb 5 oz beef chuck steak

*1 dried chipotle chilli, soaked in
 boiling water for 20 minutes*

1 garlic clove, crushed

1 tsp ground cumin

*400 g/14 oz canned chopped
 tomatoes*

8 tortillas

salt and pepper (optional)

*soured cream and green salad,
 to serve*

1. Heat the oil in a frying pan, add the onion and fry for 3–4 minutes, until golden. Tip into the slow cooker and arrange the beef on top. Drain and chop the chilli. Sprinkle over the meat with the garlic, cumin, tomatoes, and salt and pepper, if using.

2. Cover and cook on low for 4 hours until the meat is tender.

3. Warm the tortillas. Remove the beef and shred with a fork. Divide between the tortillas and spoon over the sauce. Add some soured cream and green salad, wrap and serve.

BEEF IN BEER

INGREDIENTS

4 tbsp sunflower oil

1 kg/2 lb 4 oz topside of beef, in one piece

1.5 kg/3 lb 5 oz red onions, thinly sliced

500 ml/18 fl oz beef stock

1½ tbsp plain flour

350 ml/12 fl oz beer

3 garlic cloves, chopped

1 strip thinly pared lemon rind

1 bay leaf

2 tbsp molasses

salt and pepper (optional)

fresh flat-leaf parsley sprigs, to garnish

1. Heat the oil in a large frying pan. Add the beef and cook over a medium–high heat, turning occasionally, for 5–8 minutes until brown all over. Transfer the beef to the slow cooker.

2. Reduce the heat to low and add the onions to the pan. Cook, stirring occasionally, for 5 minutes until soft. Stir in 2 tablespoons of the stock, scraping up the sediment from the base of the pan, and cook until all the liquid has evaporated. Add 2 tablespoons of the remaining stock and cook for a further 15 minutes, adding 2 tablespoons of stock when the previous addition has evaporated.

3. Stir in the flour and cook, stirring constantly, for 1 minute, then gradually stir in the remaining stock and the beer. Increase the heat to medium and bring to the boil, stirring constantly.

4. Stir in the garlic, lemon rind, bay leaf and molasses and season to taste with salt and pepper, if using. Transfer the onion mixture to the slow cooker, cover and cook on low for 8–9 hours until the beef is cooked to your liking. Remove and discard the bay leaf and serve immediately, garnished with parsley sprigs.

BEEF STEW

SERVES: 6 | **PREP:** 25 mins | **COOK:** 8 hours 30 mins–9 hours 30 mins

INGREDIENTS

4 tbsp plain flour

1 kg/2 lb 4 oz braising steak, cut
    into 4-cm/1½-inch cubes

2 tbsp sunflower oil

85 g/3 oz bacon, diced

55 g/2 oz butter

2 onions, thinly sliced

4 carrots, sliced

600 g/1 lb 5 oz potatoes, cut into
    chunks

115 g/4 oz mushrooms, sliced

1 bay leaf

2 fresh thyme sprigs, finely chopped,
    plus extra sprigs to garnish

1 tbsp finely chopped fresh parsley

400 g/14 oz canned chopped
    tomatoes

350 ml/12 fl oz beef stock

salt and pepper (optional)

1. Put the flour into a polythene bag and season to taste with salt and pepper, if using. Add the steak cubes, in batches, hold the top securely and shake well to coat. Transfer the meat to a plate.

2. Heat the oil in a large frying pan. Add the bacon and cook over a low heat, stirring frequently, for 5 minutes. Add the steak cubes, increase the heat to medium and cook, stirring frequently, for 8–10 minutes until brown all over. Remove the meat with a slotted spoon and set aside on a plate.

3. Wipe out the pan with kitchen paper, then return to a low heat and melt the butter. Add the onions and cook, stirring occasionally, for 5 minutes until soft. Add the carrots, potatoes and mushrooms and cook, stirring occasionally, for a further 5 minutes.

4. Season to taste with salt and pepper, if using, add the bay leaf, chopped thyme, parsley and tomatoes and pour in the stock. Bring to the boil, stirring occasionally, then remove the pan from the heat and transfer the mixture to the slow cooker. Stir in the meat, cover and cook on low for 8–9 hours. Remove and discard the bay leaf. Garnish with thyme sprigs and serve immediately.

SHREDDED BEEF &
PEARL BARLEY STEW

SERVES: *6* | **PREP:** *30 mins* | **COOK:** *7 hours 10 mins*

INGREDIENTS

25 g/1 oz dried ceps

350 ml/12 fl oz boiling water

1 kg/2 lb 4 oz rolled beef brisket

2 tbsp vegetable oil

2 onions, finely chopped

3 garlic cloves, sliced

½ tsp crushed dried chillies

25 g/1 oz butter

150 g/5½ oz pearl barley

3 fresh rosemary sprigs

500 ml/18 fl oz hot beef stock

salt and pepper (optional)

*2 tbsp chopped fresh parsley, to
   garnish*

steamed vegetables, to serve

1. Soak the ceps in the boiling water for 30 minutes. Remove the
mushrooms, reserving the liquid, and squeeze them dry in your
hands. Finely chop the mushrooms and set aside.

2. Season the brisket well with salt and pepper, if using. Heat the oil
in a large frying pan and, using tongs to steady the meat, brown the
beef all over for about 6–8 minutes.

3. Place the onion, garlic, chillies, butter, barley and ceps in the slow
cooker. Nestle the beef in the centre and add the rosemary sprigs.
Pour the cep soaking water and stock around the meat. Cover and
cook on high for 7 hours, or until the beef is really tender.

4. Just before serving, shred the brisket using two forks and return
it to the pot, mixing it in well. Transfer the stew to shallow bowls,
garnish with parsley and serve with steamed vegetables.

BEEF ROULADES WITH SPINACH & FETA CHEESE

INGREDIENTS

4 chuck steaks, about 675 g/
*   1 lb 8 oz in total, pounded to a*
*   thickness of 1 cm/½ inch*
½ onion, diced
115 g/4 oz feta cheese, crumbled
25 g/1 oz stoned Kalamata olives,
*   chopped*
4 small handfuls baby spinach
*   leaves*
50 ml/2 fl oz beef stock
salt and pepper (optional)

1. Season the steaks on both sides with salt and pepper, if using. Top each steak with a quarter each of the onion, cheese, olives and spinach. Starting with one of the short sides, roll up the steaks into pinwheels and secure with kitchen string or wooden cocktail sticks.

2. Place the steak rolls in the slow cooker along with the stock, and cook on high for about 3 hours or on low for 6 hours until the meat is tender and cooked through. Serve immediately.

SPRINGTIME LAMB WITH ASPARAGUS

SERVES: *4* | **PREP:** *20 mins* | **COOK:** *7 hours 35 mins–7 hours 40 mins*

INGREDIENTS

2 tbsp sunflower oil

1 onion, thinly sliced

2 garlic cloves, very finely chopped

1 kg/2 lb 4 oz boneless shoulder
of lamb, cut into 2.5-cm/1-inch
cubes

225 g/8 oz asparagus spears,
thawed if frozen

300 ml/10 fl oz chicken stock

4 tbsp lemon juice

150 ml/5 fl oz double cream

salt and pepper (optional)

1. Heat the oil in a large, heavy-based frying pan. Add the onion and cook over a medium heat, stirring occasionally, for 5 minutes until soft. Add the garlic and lamb and cook, stirring occasionally, for a further 5 minutes until brown all over.

2. Meanwhile, cut off and reserve the tips of the asparagus spears. Cut the stalks into 2–3 pieces. Add the stock and lemon juice to the pan, season with salt and pepper, if using, and bring to the boil. Reduce the heat, add the asparagus stalks and simmer for 2 minutes.

3. Transfer the mixture to the slow cooker. Cover and cook on low for 7 hours until the lamb is tender.

4. About 20 minutes before serving, cook the reserved asparagus. Add a little salt, if using, to a saucepan of water and bring to the boil. Add the asparagus tips and cook for 5 minutes. Drain well, then mix with the cream. Spoon the cream mixture on top of the lamb mixture but do not stir it in. Re-cover and cook on high for 15–20 minutes to heat through before serving.

LAMB TAGINE

INGREDIENTS

950 g/2 lb 2 oz shoulder or leg of
lamb, cut into 2.5-cm/1-inch
cubes
2 onions, roughly chopped
4-cm/1½-inch piece fresh ginger,
grated
3 garlic cloves, halved
2 tsp ground coriander
1 tsp ground cumin
1 tsp ground allspice
125 g/4½ oz Medjool dates, halved
and stoned
1 tbsp clear honey
400 g/14 oz canned chopped
tomatoes
zest of 1 lemon
1 whole cinnamon stick
150 ml/5 fl oz hot lamb stock
2 tbsp chopped fresh coriander, to
garnish
cooked couscous, to serve

1. Place the lamb, onions, ginger, garlic, ground coriander, cumin, allspice and dates in the slow cooker. Drizzle over the honey and add the tomatoes and most of the lemon zest. Add the cinnamon stick and pour over the hot stock.

2. Cover the slow cooker and cook on low for 7 hours, until the lamb is falling apart. Add a little hot water to the tagine, if needed.

3. Transfer to warmed plates, garnish with the remaining lemon zest and the fresh coriander and serve with the couscous.

LAMB STEW WITH ARTICHOKE & ROSEMARY

SERVES: *4* | **PREP:** *20 mins* | **COOK:** *5 hours 30 mins*

INGREDIENTS

1 tbsp olive oil

900 g/2 lb lamb shoulder, cut into
*   3-cm/1¼-inch cubes*

1 large onion, sliced

4 garlic cloves, thinly sliced

300 ml/10 fl oz red wine

2 tbsp red wine vinegar

1 tbsp tomato purée

10 g/¼ oz chopped fresh rosemary

400 g/14 oz canned chopped
*   tomatoes*

400 g/14 oz artichoke hearts,
*   chargrilled or in brine*

zest from 1 lemon

2 tbsp lemon juice

400 g/14 oz canned cannellini
*   beans, drained*

salt and pepper (optional)

2 tbsp chopped fresh parsley, to
*   garnish*

wholegrain mustard mash, made
*   from 1 kg/2 lb 4 oz potatoes and*
*   8 tsp mustard, to serve*

1. Heat the oil in a large frying pan over a high heat. Add the lamb in batches and cook, turning, using tongs to steady the meat, for about 8–10 minutes until brown all over. Transfer to the slow cooker.

2. Add a little more oil to the pan, if needed, then add the onion and cook over a low heat for 3–4 minutes until soft, adding the garlic for the final minute. Add the wine and cook for around 5–6 minutes until reduced by half, then transfer the mixture to the slow cooker.

3. Add the vinegar, tomato purée, rosemary and tomatoes to the slow cooker and mix well. Season with salt and pepper, if using. Re-cover and cook on high for 4 hours.

4. Add the artichokes, lemon zest, lemon juice and beans to the slow cooker. Cover and cook on high for 1 hour. Transfer to warmed serving bowls, garnish with parsley and serve with the mustard mash.

LAMB WITH
SPRING VEGETABLES

SERVES: *4–6* | **PREP:** *25 mins* | **COOK:** *9–11 hours*

INGREDIENTS

5 tbsp olive oil

6 shallots, chopped

1 garlic clove, chopped

2 celery sticks, chopped

2 tbsp plain flour

*700 g/1 lb 9 oz boned leg or
    shoulder of lamb, cut into
    2.5-cm/1-inch cubes*

850 ml/1½ pints chicken stock

115 g/4 oz pearl barley, rinsed

225 g/8 oz small turnips, halved

225 g/8 oz baby carrots

*225 g/8 oz frozen petits pois,
    thawed*

*225 g/8 oz frozen baby broad beans,
    thawed*

salt and pepper (optional)

chopped fresh parsley, to garnish

1. Heat 3 tablespoons of the oil in a large saucepan. Add the shallots, garlic and celery and cook over a low heat, stirring occasionally, for 8–10 minutes until soft and lightly browned.

2. Meanwhile, put the flour into a polythene bag and season well with salt and pepper, if using. Add the lamb cubes, in batches, and shake well to coat. Transfer the meat to a plate.

3. Using a slotted spoon, transfer the vegetables to the slow cooker. Add the remaining oil to the pan. Add the lamb, in batches if necessary, increase the heat to medium and cook, stirring frequently, for 8–10 minutes until brown all over.

4. Return all the lamb to the pan. Gradually stir in the stock, scraping up the sediment from the base of the pan. Stir in the barley, turnips and carrots, season to taste with salt and pepper, if using, and bring to the boil. Transfer the mixture to the slow cooker and stir well. Cover and cook on low for 8–10 hours until the lamb is tender.

5. Sprinkle the petits pois and broad beans on top of the stew, re-cover and cook for a further 30 minutes. Stir well, garnish with the parsley and serve immediately.

CHAPTER FOUR

FISH & SEAFOOD

RED THAI CURRY WITH SALMON & LIME

SERVES: *4* | **PREP:** *15 mins* | **COOK:** *2 hours*

INGREDIENTS

600 g/1 lb 5 oz salmon steaks,
  skinned and cut into 2–3-cm/
  ¾–1¼-inch pieces
3 tbsp red curry paste
400 ml/14 fl oz full-fat coconut milk
1 tbsp fish sauce
1 tbsp soft light brown sugar
200 g/7 oz French beans, topped
  but not tailed
1 green chilli, halved lengthways
4-cm/1½-inch piece fresh ginger,
  finely grated
100 g/3½ oz frozen peas
juice of 1 lime
3 tbsp chopped fresh coriander, to
  garnish
cooked black rice, to serve

1. Place the salmon, red curry paste, coconut milk, fish sauce, sugar, French beans, chilli and ginger in the slow cooker.

2. Cover the slow cooker and cook on high for 1 hour 30 minutes. Add the peas and cook for a further 20–30 minutes, until the peas are tender. Taste the curry and add a little more fish sauce, to taste.

3. Squeeze the lime juice over the curry and garnish with coriander. Serve immediately with black rice.

SALMON WITH LEEKS & CREAM

SERVES: *4* | **PREP:** *20–25 mins* | **COOK:** *2 hours 15 mins*

INGREDIENTS

vegetable oil, for oiling
2 tbsp butter
*2 leeks, white and light green parts
   halved lengthways, then thinly
   sliced crossways*
50 ml/2 fl oz dry white wine
125 ml/4 fl oz double cream
1 tsp salt
½ tsp pepper
*4 salmon fillets, about 175 g/6 oz
   each*
8 small fresh sage leaves

1. Lightly brush four large squares of baking paper with oil.

2. Heat the butter in a large frying pan over a medium–high heat until melted and bubbling. Add the leeks and cook, stirring occasionally, for about 5 minutes until soft.

3. Stir in the wine and bring to the boil. Cook, stirring and scraping up any sediment from the base of the pan, for a further 3 minutes, or until most of the wine has evaporated. Stir in the cream, salt and pepper and cook, stirring, for about 2 minutes until the cream is beginning to thicken.

4. Place one salmon fillet in the centre of each prepared paper square. Top with the leek and cream mixture, then place two sage leaves on top of each portion. Fold up the packets securely, leaving a little room for the steam to circulate, then place them in the slow cooker. Cover and cook on high for about 2 hours until the salmon is cooked through.

5. To serve, carefully remove the packets from the slow cooker, open and slide the contents onto warmed plates. Serve immediately.

POACHED SALMON
WITH DILL & LIME

SERVES: *4* | **PREP:** *20 mins* | **COOK:** *4 hours 5 mins*

INGREDIENTS

3 tbsp butter, melted

1 onion, thinly sliced

450 g/1 lb potatoes, peeled and thinly sliced

100 ml/3½ fl oz hot fish stock or water

4 pieces skinless salmon fillet, about 140 g/5 oz each

juice of 1 lime

2 tbsp chopped fresh dill

salt and pepper (optional)

lime wedges, to serve

1. Brush the base of the slow cooker with 1 tablespoon of the butter. Layer the onion and potatoes in the slow cooker, sprinkling with salt and pepper between the layers, if using. Add the stock and dot with 1 tablespoon of the butter. Cover and cook on low for 3 hours.

2. Arrange the salmon over the vegetables in a single layer. Drizzle the lime juice over, sprinkle with dill, and salt and pepper to taste, if using, then pour the remaining butter on top. Re-cover and cook on low for a further 1 hour until the fish flakes easily.

3. Serve the salmon and vegetables on warmed plates with the juices spooned over and lime wedges on the side.

SALMON FLORENTINE

SERVES: *4* | **PREP:** *20 mins* | **COOK:** *1 hour 40 mins*

INGREDIENTS

150 ml/5 fl oz fish stock

225 ml/8 fl oz dry white wine

2 lemons

1 onion, thinly sliced

4 salmon fillets, about 175 g/6 oz
   each

1 bouquet garni

1.3 kg/3 lb spinach, coarse stalks
   removed

freshly grated nutmeg, to taste

175 g/6 oz unsalted butter, plus
   extra for greasing

salt and pepper (optional)

1. Lightly grease the slow cooker base with butter. Pour the stock
and wine into a saucepan and bring to the boil. Meanwhile, thinly
slice one of the lemons. Arrange half of the lemon slices and all of the
onion slices over the base of the slow cooker pot and top with the
salmon fillets. Season to taste with salt and pepper, if using, add the
bouquet garni and cover the fish with the remaining lemon slices.
Pour the hot stock mixture over the fish, cover and cook on low for
1½ hours until the fish flakes easily.

2. Meanwhile, finely grate the rind and squeeze the juice from the
remaining lemon. When the fish is nearly ready, cook the spinach
in just the water clinging to the leaves, for 3–5 minutes until wilted.
Drain well, squeezing out as much water as possible. Finely chop,
arrange on a warmed serving dish and season to taste with nutmeg,
and salt and pepper, if using.

3. Carefully lift the fish out of the slow cooker and discard the lemon
slices, onion slices and bouquet garni. Put the salmon fillets on the
bed of spinach and keep warm.

4. Melt the butter in a saucepan over a low heat. Stir in the lemon
rind and half the juice. Pour over the fish and serve immediately.

FRENCH-STYLE FISH STEW

SERVES: *4–6* | **PREP:** *30 mins, plus chilling* | **COOK:** *6 hours 45 mins*

INGREDIENTS

large pinch of saffron

1 prepared squid

900 g/2 lb mixed white fish, filleted and cut into large chunks

24 large raw prawns, peeled and deveined, heads and shells reserved

2 tbsp olive oil

1 onion, finely chopped

1 fennel bulb, thinly sliced

2 large garlic cloves

4 tbsp Pernod

1 litre/1¾ pints fish stock

400 g/14 oz canned chopped tomatoes

1 tbsp tomato purée

pinch of sugar

salt and pepper (optional)

1. Toast the saffron in a dry frying pan over a high heat for 1 minute. Set aside. Cut off and reserve the tentacles from the squid and slice the body into 5-mm/¼-inch rings. Place the seafood and fish in a bowl, cover and chill in the refrigerator until required. Tie the heads and shells of the prawns in a piece of muslin.

2. Heat the oil in a frying pan. Add the onion and fennel and cook over a low heat for 5 minutes. Crush the garlic, add to the pan and cook for 2 minutes. Remove the pan from the heat. Heat the Pernod in a saucepan, ignite and pour it over the onion and fennel, gently shaking the frying pan until the flames have died down.

3. Return the frying pan to the heat, stir in the toasted saffron, stock, tomatoes, tomato purée and sugar and season to taste with salt and pepper, if using. Bring to the boil, then transfer to the slow cooker, add the bag of prawn shells, cover and cook on low for 6 hours.

4. Remove and discard the bag of prawn shells. Add the fish and seafood to the slow cooker, cover and cook on high for 30 minutes until the fish flakes easily. Serve immediately.

HALIBUT WITH
FENNEL & OLIVES

SERVES: *4* | **PREP:** *30 mins* | **COOK:** *2 hours*

INGREDIENTS

vegetable oil, for brushing

2 tbsp olive oil

50 g/1¾ oz stoned Kalamata olives, chopped

1 garlic clove, finely chopped

1 small shallot, finely chopped

zest of 1 lemon

1 tbsp finely chopped fresh oregano

1 fennel bulb, thinly sliced

4 halibut fillets, about 175 g/6 oz each

50 ml/2 fl oz dry white wine

cooked couscous, to serve

1. Lightly brush four 30 x 30-cm/12 x 12-inch squares of baking paper with vegetable oil.

2. Put the olive oil, olives, garlic, shallot, lemon zest and oregano into a bowl and mix to combine.

3. Pile equal amounts of the fennel slices in the middle of the prepared squares of baking paper. Top each pile of fennel with a halibut fillet. Spoon the olive mixture over the fish.

4. Drizzle the wine over the fish. Fold up the packets, leaving a little room for the steam to circulate and place them in the slow cooker. Cover and cook on high for about 2 hours until cooked through.

5. To serve, open up the packets and gently transfer the contents to warmed plates. Serve immediately with couscous.

GINGER-STEAMED HALIBUT WITH TOMATOES & BEANS

SERVES: *4* | **PREP:** *25–30 mins, plus marinating* | **COOK:** *2 hours*

INGREDIENTS

1 tbsp finely chopped fresh ginger

2 garlic cloves, finely chopped

1–2 hot red chillies, deseeded and sliced

2 tbsp Thai fish sauce

2 tbsp mirin or other sweet white wine

1 tsp sugar

4 halibut fillets (about 675 g/1 lb 8 oz in total)

vegetable oil, for oiling

350 g/12 oz French beans, topped and tailed

450 g/1 lb cherry tomatoes, halved, or quartered if large

TO GARNISH

4 spring onions, thinly sliced

fresh coriander, finely chopped

fresh basil leaves, shredded

1. Put the ginger, garlic, chillies, fish sauce, mirin and sugar into a baking dish large enough to hold the fish and stir to combine. Add the fish and turn to coat in the mixture. Cover and place in the refrigerator to marinate for 30 minutes.

2. Meanwhile, brush four large squares of baking paper with oil.

3. Divide the beans evenly between the prepared squares of paper, piling them in the middle. Scatter the tomatoes evenly over them. Top each pile of vegetables with a fish fillet and some of the marinade. Fold up the packets securely, leaving a little room for the steam to circulate, and place them in the slow cooker. Cover and cook on high for 2 hours until the fish is flaky and cooked through.

4. To serve, carefully remove the packets from the slow cooker, open them and slide the contents onto warmed plates, then garnish with spring onions, coriander and basil.

POLLOCK BAKE

SERVES: *4* | **PREP:** *15 mins* | **COOK:** *2 hours 5 mins*

INGREDIENTS

1 tbsp olive oil

1 red onion, sliced

1 yellow pepper, deseeded and
  sliced

4 pollock fillets, about 140 g/5 oz
  each

2 tomatoes, thinly sliced

8 stoned black olives, halved

1 garlic clove, thinly sliced

2 tsp balsamic vinegar

juice of 1 orange

salt and pepper (optional)

1. Heat the oil in a frying pan, add the onion and yellow pepper and fry over a high heat for 3–4 minutes, stirring, until lightly browned. Transfer to the slow cooker, cover and cook on high for 1 hour.

2. Arrange the fish fillets over the vegetables and season to taste with salt and pepper, if using. Arrange a layer of tomatoes and olives over the top and sprinkle with the garlic and vinegar.

3. Pour over the orange juice, cover and cook on high for a further 1 hour. Serve immediately.

TAGLIATELLE
WITH TUNA

SERVES: *4* | **PREP:** *20 mins* | **COOK:** *2 hours 10 mins*

INGREDIENTS

200 g/7 oz dried egg tagliatelle

400 g/14 oz canned tuna steak in oil, drained

1 bunch spring onions, sliced

175 g/6 oz frozen peas

2 tsp hot chilli sauce

600 ml/1 pint hot chicken stock

115 g/4 oz grated Cheddar cheese

salt and pepper (optional)

1. Add a little salt, if using, to a large saucepan of water and bring to the boil. Add the pasta, bring back to the boil and cook for 2 minutes until the pasta ribbons are loose. Drain.

2. Break up the tuna into bite-sized chunks and place in the slow cooker with the pasta, spring onions and peas. Season to taste with salt and pepper, if using.

3. Add the chilli sauce to the stock and pour over the ingredients in the slow cooker. Sprinkle the grated cheese over the top. Cover and cook on low for 2 hours. Serve immediately on warmed plates.

RED SNAPPER
WITH FENNEL

SERVES: *4* | **PREP:** *20 mins* | **COOK:** *1 hours 30 mins–1 hours 45 mins*

INGREDIENTS

4 whole red snapper, about
  350g/12 oz each, cleaned
1 orange, halved and thinly sliced
2 garlic cloves, thinly sliced
6 fresh thyme sprigs
1 tbsp olive oil
1 fennel bulb, thinly sliced
450 ml/16 fl oz orange juice
1 bay leaf
1 tsp dill seeds
salt and pepper (optional)
salad leaves, to serve

1. Season the fish inside and outside with salt and pepper, if using. Make 3–4 diagonal slashes on each side. Divide the orange slices between the cavities and add 2–3 garlic slices and a thyme sprig to each. Put the remaining garlic and thyme in the slashes.

2. Heat the oil in a large frying pan. Add the fennel and cook over a medium heat, stirring frequently, for 3–5 minutes until just soft. Add the orange juice and bay leaf and bring to the boil, then reduce the heat and simmer for a further 5 minutes.

3. Transfer the fennel mixture to the slow cooker. Put the fish on top and sprinkle with the dill seeds. Cover and cook on high for 1¼–1½ hours, until the flesh flakes easily.

4. Carefully transfer the fish to warmed plates. Remove and discard the bay leaf. Spoon the fennel and some of the cooking juices over the fish and serve immediately with salad leaves.

SEA BREAM IN LEMON SAUCE

SERVES: *4* | **PREP:** *15 mins* | **COOK:** *1 hour 45 mins*

INGREDIENTS

8 sea bream fillets

55 g/2 oz unsalted butter

25 g/1 oz plain flour

850 ml/1½ pints warm milk

4 tbsp lemon juice

225 g/8 oz mushrooms, sliced

1 bouquet garni

salt and pepper (optional)

*lemon wedges and griddled
    asparagus, to serve*

1. Put the fish fillets into the slow cooker and set aside.

2. Melt the butter in a saucepan over a low heat. Add the flour and cook, stirring constantly, for 1 minute. Gradually stir in the milk, a little at a time, and bring to the boil, stirring constantly. Stir in the lemon juice and mushrooms, add the bouquet garni and season to taste with salt and pepper, if using. Reduce the heat and simmer for 5 minutes. Pour the sauce over the fish fillets, cover and cook on low for 1½ hours.

3. Carefully lift out the fish fillets and transfer to warmed serving plates. Serve immediately with lemon wedges and asparagus.

PRAWN BISQUE

SERVES: *4–6* | **PREP:** *25–30 mins* | **COOK:** *3 hours 40 mins–6 hours 40 mins*

INGREDIENTS

1 tbsp butter

1 onion, diced

100 g/3½ oz long-grain rice

2 tbsp tomato purée

1½ tsp salt

½ tsp cayenne pepper

2 litres/3½ pints low-sodium prawn stock or fish stock

1 carrot, diced

1 celery stick, diced

225 g/8 oz mushrooms, diced

675 g/1 lb 8 oz raw prawns, peeled, deveined and cut into bite-sized pieces, if large

150 ml/5 fl oz double cream

2 tbsp lemon juice

snipped fresh chives, to garnish

1. Melt the butter in a large frying pan over a medium–high heat. Add the onion and cook, stirring, for about 5 minutes until soft. Add the rice, tomato purée, salt and cayenne pepper and cook, stirring, for a further 1 minute. Add a quarter of the stock and cook, stirring, for about a further 1 minute, scraping up any sediment from the base of the pan.

2. Add the onion mixture to the slow cooker together with the carrot, celery, mushrooms and remaining stock. Cover and cook on high for 3 hours or on low for 6 hours.

3. Using a food processor or blender, purée the soup in batches. Return to the slow cooker, add the prawns, cover and cook on high for 30 minutes until the prawns are cooked through. Stir in the cream and lemon juice and serve immediately, garnished with chives.

PASTA & PRAWNS

SERVES: *4* | **PREP:** *15 mins* | **COOK:** *7 hours 15 mins*

INGREDIENTS

*400 g/14 oz tomatoes, peeled and
  chopped*
140 g/5 oz tomato purée
1 garlic clove, finely chopped
2 tbsp chopped fresh parsley
*500 g/1 lb 2 oz cooked, peeled
  Mediterranean prawns*
6 fresh basil leaves, torn
400 g/14 oz dried tagliatelle
salt and pepper (optional)
fresh basil leaves, to garnish

1. Put the tomatoes, tomato purée, garlic and parsley in the slow cooker and season with salt and pepper, if using. Cover and cook on low for 7 hours.

2. Add the prawns and basil to the slow cooker. Re-cover and cook on high for 15 minutes.

3. Meanwhile, add a little salt, if using, to a large saucepan of water and bring to the boil. Add the pasta, bring back to the boil and cook for 10–12 minutes until tender but still firm to the bite.

4. Drain the pasta and tip it into a warmed serving bowl. Add the prawn sauce and toss lightly with two large forks. Garnish with basil leaves and serve immediately.

NEW ENGLAND
CLAM CHOWDER

SERVES: *4* | **PREP:** *20 mins* | **COOK:** *4 hours 5 mins*

INGREDIENTS

25 g/1 oz butter

1 onion, finely chopped

2 potatoes, peeled and cut into
  cubes

1 large carrot, diced

400 ml/14 fl oz fish stock or water

280 g/10 oz canned clams, drained

250 ml/9 fl oz double cream

salt and pepper (optional)

chopped fresh parsley, to garnish

fresh crusty bread, to serve

1. Melt the butter in a frying pan, add the onion and fry over a medium heat, stirring, for 4–5 minutes until golden.

2. Transfer the onion to the slow cooker with the potatoes, carrot, stock and salt and pepper to taste, if using. Cover and cook on high for 3 hours.

3. Add the clams and the cream to the slow cooker and stir to mix evenly. Re-cover and cook for a further 1 hour.

4. Serve the chowder immediately, garnished with parsley and served with fresh crusty bread.

LOUISIANA GUMBO

SERVES: 6 | **PREP:** 25–30 mins | **COOK:** 5 hours 50 mins–6 hours 50 mins

INGREDIENTS

2 tbsp sunflower oil

175 g/6 oz okra, cut into 2.5-cm/
   1-inch pieces

2 onions, finely chopped

4 celery sticks, very finely chopped

1 garlic clove, finely chopped

2 tbsp plain flour

½ tsp sugar

1 tsp ground cumin

700 ml/1¼ pints fish stock

1 red pepper, deseeded and
   chopped

1 green pepper, deseeded and
   chopped

2 large tomatoes, chopped

4 tbsp chopped fresh parsley

1 tbsp chopped fresh coriander

hot pepper sauce, to taste

350 g/12 oz large raw prawns,
   peeled and deveined

350 g/12 oz cod or haddock fillets,
   skinned and cut into 2.5-cm/
   1-inch chunks

350 g/12 oz monkfish fillet, cut into
   2.5-cm/1-inch chunks

salt and pepper (optional)

1. Heat half the oil in a heavy-based frying pan. Add the okra and cook over a low heat, stirring frequently, for 5 minutes until brown. Using a slotted spoon, transfer the okra to the slow cooker.

2. Add the remaining oil to the pan. Add the onions and celery and cook over a low heat, stirring occasionally, for 5 minutes until soft. Add the garlic and cook, stirring frequently, for 1 minute, then sprinkle in the flour, sugar and cumin, and season to taste with salt and pepper, if using. Cook, stirring constantly, for 2 minutes, then remove the pan from the heat.

3. Gradually stir in the stock, then return the pan to the heat and bring to the boil, stirring constantly. Pour the mixture over the okra and stir in the red and green peppers and tomatoes. Cover and cook on low for 5–6 hours.

4. Stir in the parsley, coriander and hot pepper sauce to taste, then add the prawns, cod and monkfish. Cover and cook on high for 30 minutes until the fish is cooked and the prawns have changed colour. Serve immediately.

EASY BOUILLABAISSE

SERVES: *4* | **PREP:** *30 mins* | **COOK:** *2 hours 30 mins–4 hours 30 mins*

INGREDIENTS

pinch of saffron threads

1 tbsp hot water

2 tbsp olive oil

1 onion, diced

3 garlic cloves, finely chopped

2 celery sticks, finely chopped

1 tsp salt

¼–½ tsp dried red pepper flakes

350 ml/12 fl oz dry white wine

400 g/14 oz canned tomato purée

400 g/14 oz canned chopped
  tomatoes, with juice

12 small live clams, scrubbed

12 live mussels, scrubbed and
  debearded

450 g/1 lb white fish fillet, cut into
  5-cm/2-inch pieces

225 g/8 oz raw prawns, peeled and
  deveined

2 tbsp finely chopped fresh parsley,
  to garnish

aïoli, to serve

1. Place the saffron in a small bowl and cover with the hot water. Heat the oil in a large frying pan over a medium–high heat. Add the onion and garlic and cook, stirring, for about 5 minutes until soft. Add the celery, salt and red pepper flakes, then add the wine. Bring to the boil and cook, stirring, for about 8 minutes until the liquid is reduced by half. Transfer the mixture to the slow cooker.

2. Stir in the saffron and its soaking water, tomato purée and tomatoes with their can juices. Cover and cook on high for about 2 hours or on low for about 4 hours.

3. Discard any clams or mussels with broken shells and any that refuse to close when tapped. Add the fish, prawns, clams and mussels, re-cover and cook on high for a further 10–15 minutes until the fish and prawns are cooked through and the clams and mussels have opened, discarding any that still remain closed.

4. To serve, ladle some broth into four serving bowls, then add some of the fish and shellfish. Top each serving with a dollop of aïoli, garnish with parsley and serve immediately.

CLAMS IN SPICY BROTH WITH CHORIZO

SERVES: *4* | **PREP:** *25 mins* | **COOK:** *2 hours 25 mins–4 hours 25 mins*

INGREDIENTS

1 tbsp olive oil

1 red onion, halved lengthways and sliced

115 g/4 oz chorizo sausage, diced

1 fennel bulb, roughly chopped

400 g/14 oz canned chopped tomatoes

125 ml/4 fl oz dry white wine

125 ml/4 fl oz clam juice or water

½ tsp salt

¼–½ tsp crushed red pepper flakes

900 g/2 lb small live clams, scrubbed

2 tbsp chopped fresh flat-leaf parsley, to garnish

1. Heat the oil in a large frying pan over a medium–high heat. Add the onion and cook, stirring, for about 5 minutes until soft. Add the chorizo and continue to cook, stirring occasionally, until the meat begins to brown. Transfer the mixture to the slow cooker.

2. Stir in the fennel, tomatoes and their can juices, wine, clam juice, salt and red pepper flakes. Cover and cook on high for about 2 hours or on low for about 4 hours.

3. Discard any clams with broken shells and any that refuse to close when tapped. Add the clams to the slow cooker, re-cover and cook on high for a further 10–15 minutes until the clams have opened. Discard any clams that remain closed.

4. Serve the clams in bowls, with a generous amount of broth and garnished with parsley.

SEAFOOD IN SAFFRON SAUCE

SERVES: *4* | **PREP:** *20 mins* | **COOK:** *5 hours 45 mins*

INGREDIENTS

2 tbsp olive oil

1 onion, sliced

pinch of saffron threads

1 tbsp chopped fresh thyme

2 garlic cloves, finely chopped

800 g/1 lb 12 oz canned chopped tomatoes

175 ml/6 fl oz dry white wine

2 litres/3½ pints fish stock

225 g/8 oz live clams, scrubbed

225 g/8 oz live mussels, scrubbed and debearded

350 g/12 oz red mullet fillets

450 g/1 lb monkfish fillets

225 g/8 oz squid rings, thawed if frozen

2 tbsp shredded fresh basil

salt and pepper (optional)

1. Heat the oil in a heavy-based frying pan. Add the onion, saffron, thyme and a pinch of salt, if using, and cook over a low heat, stirring occasionally, for 5 minutes until soft. Add the garlic and cook, stirring constantly, for 2 minutes.

2. Drain and add the tomatoes, wine and stock, season to taste with salt and pepper, if using, and bring to the boil, stirring constantly. Transfer the mixture to the slow cooker, then cover and cook on low for 5 hours.

3. Discard any clams or mussels with broken shells and any that refuse to close when tapped. Cut the mullet and monkfish fillets into bite-sized chunks.

4. Add the fish pieces, clams, mussels and squid rings to the slow cooker, re-cover and cook on high for 30 minutes until the clams and mussels have opened and the fish is cooked through. Discard any shellfish that remain closed. Stir in the basil and serve immediately.

SOUTH-WESTERN SEAFOOD STEW

SERVES: *4* | **PREP:** *25 mins* | **COOK:** *8 hours 15 mins*

INGREDIENTS

*2 tbsp olive oil, plus extra for
    drizzling*

1 large onion, chopped

4 garlic cloves finely chopped

*1 yellow pepper, deseeded and
    chopped*

*1 red pepper, deseeded and
    chopped*

*1 orange pepper, deseeded and
    chopped*

*450 g/1 lb tomatoes, peeled and
    chopped*

*2 large mild green chillies, such as
    poblano, chopped*

*finely grated rind and juice of
    1 lime*

*2 tbsp chopped fresh coriander, plus
    extra leaves to garnish*

1 bay leaf

*450 ml/16 fl oz fish, vegetable or
    chicken stock*

450 g/1 lb red mullet fillets

450 g/1 lb raw prawns

225 g/8 oz prepared squid

salt and pepper (optional)

1. Heat the oil in a saucepan. Add the onion and garlic and cook over a low heat, stirring occasionally, for 5 minutes until soft. Add the yellow, red and orange peppers, tomatoes and chillies and cook, stirring frequently, for a further 5 minutes. Stir in the lime rind and juice, add the chopped coriander and bay leaf and pour in the stock. Bring to the boil, stirring occasionally.

2. Transfer the mixture to the slow cooker, cover and cook on low for 7½ hours. Meanwhile, skin the fish fillets, if necessary, and cut the flesh into chunks. Peel and devein the prawns. Cut the squid bodies into rings and halve the tentacles or leave them whole.

3. Add the seafood to the stew, season with salt and pepper, if using, re-cover and cook on high for 30 minutes, or until tender and cooked through. Remove and discard the bay leaf. Transfer to warmed serving bowls, garnish with coriander leaves and serve immediately.

JAMBALAYA

SERVES: *4* | **PREP:** *25 mins* | **COOK:** *6 hours 45 mins*

INGREDIENTS

½ tsp cayenne pepper

½ tsp pepper

1 tsp salt

2 tsp chopped fresh thyme

350 g/12 oz skinless, boneless
   chicken breasts, diced

2 tbsp corn oil

2 onions, chopped

2 garlic cloves, finely chopped

2 green peppers, deseeded and
   chopped

2 celery sticks, chopped

115 g/4 oz smoked ham, chopped

175 g/6 oz chorizo sausage, sliced

400 g/14 oz canned chopped
   tomatoes

2 tbsp tomato purée

225 ml/8 fl oz chicken stock

450 g/1 lb raw prawns, peeled and
   deveined

450 g/1 lb cooked rice

snipped fresh chives, to garnish

1. Mix the cayenne pepper, pepper, salt and thyme together in a bowl. Add the chicken and toss to coat.

2. Heat the oil in a large, heavy-based saucepan. Add the onions, garlic, green peppers and celery and cook over a low heat, stirring occasionally, for 5 minutes. Add the chicken and cook over a medium heat, stirring frequently, for a further 5 minutes until golden all over. Stir in the ham, chorizo, tomatoes, tomato purée and stock and bring to the boil.

3. Transfer the mixture to the slow cooker. Cover and cook on low for 6 hours. Add the prawns and rice, then re-cover and cook on high for 30 minutes.

4. Transfer to warmed plates, garnish with chives and serve immediately.

CHAPTER FIVE

DESSERTS

APPLE, PLUM & ALMOND COMPOTE

SERVES: *6* | **PREP:** *20 mins* | **COOK:** *3 hours*

INGREDIENTS

1.3 kg/3 lb cooking apples, peeled, cored and roughly chopped

600 g/1 lb 5 oz plums, stoned and quartered

50 g/1¾ oz soft light brown sugar

1 tsp vanilla extract

1 tsp almond extract

50 g/1¾ oz flaked almonds, toasted, to decorate

1. Place the apples, plums, sugar, vanilla extract and almond extract in the slow cooker.

2. Cover the slow cooker and cook on high for 3 hours, then stir the contents to break down any remaining chunks of apple.

3. Serve hot, warm or cold with a sprinkling of flaked almonds.

CHOCOLATE &
WALNUT SPONGE

SERVES: *4* | **PREP:** *25 mins* | **COOK:** *3 hours–3 hours 30 minutes*

INGREDIENTS

55 g/2 oz cocoa powder, plus extra
  for dusting
2 tbsp milk
115 g/4 oz self-raising flour
pinch of salt
115 g/4 oz unsalted butter, softened,
  plus extra for greasing
115 g/4 oz caster sugar
2 eggs, lightly beaten
55 g/2 oz walnut halves, chopped
whipped cream, to serve

1. Grease a 1.2-litre/2-pint pudding basin with butter. Cut out a double round of greaseproof paper 7 cm/2¾ inches wider than the rim of the basin. Grease one side of the paper with butter and make a pleat in the centre.

2. Mix the cocoa and the milk to a paste in a small bowl. Sift together the flour and salt into a separate small bowl. Set aside.

3. Beat together the butter and sugar in a large bowl until pale and fluffy. Gradually beat in the eggs, a little at a time, then gently fold in the flour mixture, followed by the cocoa mixture and the walnuts.

4. Spoon the mixture into the prepared basin. Cover the basin with the greaseproof paper rounds, buttered-side down, and tie in place with string. Stand the basin on a trivet or rack in the slow cooker and pour in enough boiling water to come about halfway up the side of the basin. Cover and cook on high for 3–3½ hours.

5. Remove the basin from the slow cooker and discard the greaseproof paper. Run a knife around the inside of the basin, then turn out onto a warmed serving dish. Serve with whipped cream, dusted with cocoa.

RICE PUDDING

SERVES: *4* | **PREP:** *15 mins* | **COOK:** *2 hours 15 minutes–2 hours 20 mins*

INGREDIENTS

140 g/5 oz short-grain rice

1 litre/1¾ pints milk

115 g/4 oz sugar

1 tsp vanilla extract

ground cinnamon, for dusting

1. Rinse the rice well under cold running water and drain thoroughly. Pour the milk into a large, heavy-based saucepan, add the sugar and bring to the boil, stirring constantly. Sprinkle in the rice, stir well and simmer gently for 10–15 minutes. Transfer the mixture to a heatproof dish and cover with foil.

2. Stand the dish on a trivet or rack in the slow cooker and pour in enough boiling water to come about one third of the way up the side of the dish. Cover and cook on high for 2 hours.

3. Remove the dish from the slow cooker and discard the foil. Stir the vanilla extract into the rice, then spoon it into warmed bowls. Lightly dust with cinnamon and serve immediately.

BUTTERSCOTCH PUDDINGS

SERVES: 6 | **PREP:** 20 mins, plus cooling & chilling | **COOK:** 2 hours 5 mins

INGREDIENTS

2 tbsp unsalted butter

275 g/9¾ oz soft dark brown sugar

½ tsp salt

300 ml/10 fl oz double cream

175 ml/6 fl oz milk

4 egg yolks, lightly beaten

2 tsp vanilla extract

2 tsp whisky

whipped cream, to serve

1. Fill the slow cooker with water to a depth of 4 cm/1½ inches.

2. Melt the butter in a large saucepan over a medium heat. Add the sugar and salt and stir to mix well. Add the cream and milk and heat over a medium heat until hot but not boiling.

3. Place the egg yolks in a mixing bowl. Add the sugar and milk mixture in a very thin stream, whisking constantly. Whisk in the vanilla extract and whisky, then ladle the mixture into six 125-ml/4-fl oz ramekins.

4. Carefully place the ramekins in the slow cooker, taking care not to slosh any of the water into them. Cover the slow cooker and cook on low for about 2 hours, or until the puddings are set.

5. Remove the ramekins from the slow cooker and transfer to a wire rack to cool for about 15 minutes, then cover with clingfilm, place in the refrigerator and chill for at least 2 hours before serving. Serve chilled, topped with a dollop of whipped cream.

ITALIAN
BREAD PUDDING

SERVES: *4* | **PREP:** *20 mins, plus cooling & chilling* | **COOK:** *2 hours 35 mins*

INGREDIENTS

unsalted butter, for greasing
6 slices panettone
3 tbsp Marsala
300 ml/10 fl oz milk
300 ml/10 fl oz single cream
100 g/3½ oz caster sugar
grated rind of ½ lemon
pinch of ground cinnamon
3 large eggs, lightly beaten

1. Grease a pudding basin and set aside. Place the panettone on a deep plate and sprinkle with the Marsala.

2. Pour the milk and cream into a saucepan and add the sugar, lemon rind and cinnamon. Gradually bring to the boil over a low heat, stirring until the sugar has dissolved. Remove the pan from the heat and leave to cool slightly, then pour the mixture onto the eggs, beating constantly.

3. Place the panettone in the prepared dish, pour in the egg mixture and cover with foil. Place in the slow cooker and add enough boiling water to come about one third of the way up the side of the dish. Cover and cook on high for 2½ hours until set.

4. Remove the dish from the slow cooker and discard the foil. Leave to cool, then chill in the refrigerator until required. Loosen the sides of the pudding and turn out onto a serving dish.

APPLE CRUMBLE

INGREDIENTS

100 g/3½ oz sugar

1 tbsp cornflour

1 tsp ground cinnamon

¼ tsp ground nutmeg

6 large cooking apples, peeled,
*   cored and chopped*

2 tbsp lemon juice

vanilla ice cream, to serve

TOPPING

60 g/2¼ oz plain flour

75 g/2¾ oz soft light brown sugar

3 tbsp granulated sugar

pinch of salt

3 tbsp unsalted butter, cut into
*   small pieces*

60 g/2¼ oz rolled oats

85 g/3 oz pecan nuts or walnuts,
*   roughly chopped*

1. Put the sugar, cornflour, cinnamon and nutmeg into the slow cooker and stir to combine. Add the apples and lemon juice and toss to coat well.

2. To make the topping, put the flour, brown sugar, granulated sugar and salt into a large mixing bowl and mix to combine. Using two knives, cut the butter into the flour mixture until it resembles coarse crumbs. Add the oats and nuts and toss until well combined.

3. Sprinkle the topping evenly over the apple mixture, cover and cook on high for about 2 hours or on low for about 4 hours until the apples are soft. Set the lid ajar and cook for a further 1 hour, or until the topping is crisp. Serve warm, topped with vanilla ice cream.

POACHED PEACHES
IN MARSALA

SERVES: *4* | **PREP:** *20 mins, plus cooling* | **COOK:** *1 hour 20 mins–1 hour 50 mins*

INGREDIENTS

150 ml/5 fl oz Marsala

175 ml/6 fl oz water

4 tbsp caster sugar

1 vanilla pod, split lengthways

6 peaches, stoned and cut into wedges, or 12 apricots, stoned and halved

2 tsp cornflour

crème fraîche or Greek-style natural yogurt, to serve

1. Pour the Marsala and 150 ml/5 fl oz of the water into a saucepan and add the sugar and vanilla pod. Set the pan over a low heat and stir until the sugar has dissolved, then bring to the boil without stirring. Remove from the heat.

2. Put the peaches into the slow cooker and pour the syrup over them. Cover and cook on high for 1–1½ hours until tender.

3. Using a slotted spoon, gently transfer the peaches to a serving dish. Remove the vanilla pod from the slow cooker and scrape the seeds into the syrup with the point of a knife. Discard the pod. Stir the cornflour to a paste with the remaining water in a small bowl, then stir into the syrup. Re-cover and cook on high for 15 minutes, stirring occasionally.

4. Spoon the syrup over the fruit and leave to cool slightly. Serve warm or chill in the refrigerator for 2 hours before serving with crème fraîche or yogurt.

BLUSHING PEARS

SERVES: 6 | **PREP:** *20 mins, plus cooling & chilling* | **COOK:** *4 hours*

INGREDIENTS

6 small ripe pears

225 ml/8 fl oz ruby port

200 g/7 oz caster sugar

1 tsp finely chopped crystallized ginger

2 tbsp lemon juice

whipped cream or Greek-style natural yogurt, to serve

1. Peel the pears, cut them in half lengthways and scoop out the cores. Place them in the slow cooker.

2. Combine the port, sugar, ginger and lemon juice in a jug and pour the mixture over the pears. Cover and cook on low for 4 hours until the pears are tender.

3. Leave the pears to cool in the slow cooker, then carefully transfer to a bowl and chill in the refrigerator until required.

4. To serve, cut each pear half into about six slices lengthways, leaving the fruit intact at the stalk end. Carefully lift the pear halves onto serving plates and press gently to fan out the slices. Spoon the cooking juices over the pears and serve with whipped cream.

CRÈME BRÛLÉE

SERVES: *6* | **PREP:** *20 mins, plus infusing, cooling & chilling* | **COOK:** *3 hours 5 mins–3 hours 35 mins*

INGREDIENTS

1 vanilla pod

1 litre/1¾ pints double cream

6 egg yolks

100 g/3½ oz caster sugar

85 g/3 oz soft light brown sugar

1. Using a sharp knife, split the vanilla pod in half lengthways, scrape the seeds into a saucepan and add the pod. Pour in the cream and bring just to the boil, stirring constantly. Remove from the heat, cover and leave to infuse for 20 minutes.

2. Whisk together the egg yolks and caster sugar in a bowl until thoroughly mixed. Remove the vanilla pod from the pan and discard, then whisk the cream into the egg yolk mixture. Strain the mixture into a large jug.

3. Divide the mixture between six ramekins and cover with foil. Stand the ramekins on a trivet or rack in the slow cooker and pour in enough boiling water to come about halfway up the sides of the ramekins. Cover and cook on low for 3–3½ hours until just set. Remove the slow cooker pot from the base of the slow cooker and leave to cool completely, then remove the ramekins and chill in the refrigerator for at least 4 hours.

4. Preheat the grill. Sprinkle the brown sugar evenly over the surface of each dessert, then cook under the grill for 30–60 seconds until the sugar has melted and caramelized. Alternatively, you can use a cook's blowtorch. Chill for a further hour before serving.

CHOCOLATE FONDUE

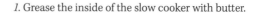

SERVES: *4–6* | **PREP:** *15 mins* | **COOK:** *45 mins–1 hour*

INGREDIENTS

butter, for greasing

225 ml/8 fl oz double cream

350 g/12 oz plain chocolate,
*   chopped into small pieces*

1 tsp vanilla extract

TO SERVE

diced fruit (bananas, strawberries,
*   apples, pears)*

marshmallows

cookies or pieces of cake

1. Grease the inside of the slow cooker with butter.

2. Put the cream and chocolate into the slow cooker and stir to combine. Cover and cook on low, stirring occasionally, for 45 minutes–1 hour until the chocolate is completely melted. Stir in the vanilla extract.

3. Leave the mixture in the slow cooker or transfer to a fondue pot with a burner and serve immediately, with platters of diced fruit, marshmallows and cookies for dipping.

STUFFED APPLES

SERVES: *4* | **PREP:** *20 mins* | **COOK:** *1 hour 30 minutes–3 hours*

INGREDIENTS

4 large cooking apples

175 g/6 oz soft light brown sugar

25 g/1 oz rolled oats

1 tsp ground cinnamon

4 tbsp butter, cut into small pieces

2 tbsp sultanas

25 g/1 oz pecan nuts or walnuts,
  roughly chopped

whipped cream, to serve

1. Use a paring knife to cut the stem end out of each apple, then scoop out the core with a melon baller or teaspoon, leaving the base of the apple intact.

2. To make the filling, put the sugar, oats, cinnamon and butter into a bowl and mix together with a fork. Add the sultanas and nuts and toss to mix well. Stuff the mixture into the apples, dividing it evenly.

3. Pour 125 ml/4 fl oz of water into the slow cooker, then carefully add the apples, standing them up in the base of the slow cooker. Cover and cook on high for about 1½ hours or on low for 3 hours. Serve the apples hot, topped with whipped cream.

CHOCOLATE POTS

SERVES: 6 | **PREP:** *25 mins, plus cooling & chilling* | **COOK:** *3 hours 10 mins–3 hours 40 mins*

INGREDIENTS

300 ml/10 fl oz single cream

300 ml/10 fl oz milk

225 g/8 oz plain chocolate, broken into small pieces

1 large egg

4 egg yolks

4 tbsp caster sugar

150 ml/5 fl oz double cream

grated chocolate, to decorate

1. Pour the single cream and milk into a saucepan and add the chocolate. Set the pan over a very low heat and stir until the chocolate has melted and the mixture is smooth. Remove from the heat and leave to cool for 10 minutes.

2. Beat together the egg, egg yolks and sugar in a bowl until combined. Gradually stir in the chocolate mixture until thoroughly blended, then strain into a jug.

3. Divide the mixture between six ramekins and cover with foil. Stand the ramekins on a trivet or rack in the slow cooker and pour in enough boiling water to come about halfway up the sides of the ramekins. Cover and cook on low for 3–3½ hours, until just set. Remove the slow cooker pot from the base and leave to cool completely, then remove the ramekins and chill in the refrigerator for at least 4 hours.

4. Whip the double cream in a bowl until it holds soft peaks. Top each chocolate pot with a little of the whipped cream and decorate with grated chocolate. Serve immediately.

SWEET POTATO, APPLE & RAISIN COMPOTE

SERVES: 6 | **PREP:** *15 mins* | **COOK:** *3 hours*

INGREDIENTS

*550 g/1 lb 4 oz sweet potatoes
(about 4), peeled and cut into
3-cm/1¼-inch cubes*

*800 g/1 lb 12 oz apples (about 4),
peeled and cut into 4-cm/
1½-inch cubes*

100 g/3½ oz raisins

200 ml/7 fl oz apple juice

1 tbsp clear honey

½ tsp freshly ground nutmeg

¼ tsp ground cloves

*70 g/2½ oz pecan nuts, roughly
chopped, to decorate*

whipped cream, to serve

1. Place the sweet potatoes, apples, raisins, apple juice, honey, nutmeg and cloves in the slow cooker. Cover and cook on high for 3 hours. Once cooked, stir the ingredients gently to combine them.

2. Put the compote in bowls, decorate with the pecan nuts and serve with whipped cream.

DOUBLE CHOCOLATE
BROWNIES

MAKES: *18 brownies* | **PREP:** *20 mins, plus cooling* | **COOK:** *3 hours*

INGREDIENTS

125 g/4½ oz plain flour

85 g/3 oz cocoa powder

½ tsp baking powder

¼ tsp salt

115 g/4 oz unsalted butter, plus
extra for greasing

100 g/3½ oz sugar

1 large egg

1 tsp vanilla extract

25 g/1 oz plain chocolate chips

1. Grease the inside of the slow cooker with butter.

2. Put the flour, cocoa powder, baking powder and salt into a medium-sized bowl and mix to combine. Put the butter and sugar into a large bowl and cream together. Add the egg and vanilla extract and beat well together. Gradually beat in the flour mixture until well incorporated. Stir in the chocolate chips.

3. Using a rubber spatula, scrape the batter into the prepared slow cooker and smooth the top. Cover and cook on low for 2½ hours. Set the lid slightly ajar and cook on low for a further 30 minutes.

4. Remove the slow cooker pot from the base of the slow cooker and transfer to a wire rack to cool for 30 minutes, then turn the brownie out onto the rack and leave to cool for a further 30 minutes. Slice into 5-cm/2-inch pieces and serve at room temperature.

CARROT CAKE

SERVES: *8–10* | **PREP:** *25 mins, plus cooling* | **COOK:** *2 hours*

INGREDIENTS

125 g/4½ oz plain flour
1 tsp bicarbonate of soda
¼ tsp salt
½ tsp ground cinnamon
pinch of ground nutmeg
2 large eggs
100 g/3½ oz granulated sugar
55 g/2 oz soft light brown sugar
*4 tbsp vegetable oil, plus extra for
   oiling*
150 ml/5 fl oz buttermilk
1 tsp vanilla extract
450 g/1 lb carrots, grated
60 g/2¼ oz desiccated coconut
35 g/1¼ oz sultanas
whipped cream, to serve

1. Oil the inside of the slow cooker.

2. Put the flour, bicarbonate of soda, salt, cinnamon and nutmeg into a small bowl and mix to combine. Put the eggs, granulated sugar and brown sugar into a medium-sized bowl and whisk together until well combined. Add the oil, buttermilk and vanilla extract and stir to combine. Add the egg mixture to the flour mixture and mix well. Fold in the carrots, coconut and sultanas.

3. Pour the mixture into the prepared slow cooker. Place several sheets of kitchen paper on top of the slow cooker, then put the lid on top to secure the kitchen paper in place above the cake mixture. Cook on low for about 2 hours until a skewer inserted into the centre of the cake comes out clean.

4. Remove the slow cooker pot from the base of the slow cooker and transfer to a wire rack to cool for at least 30 minutes. Cut the cake into wedges and serve directly from the pot. Serve warm or at room temperature with a dollop of whipped cream.

GINGER CAKE

SERVES: *8–10* | **PREP:** *20 mins, plus cooling* | **COOK:** *3 hours 5 mins*

INGREDIENTS

115 g/4 oz unsalted butter, melted,
 plus extra for greasing
85 g/3 oz soft light brown sugar
150 ml/5 fl oz golden syrup
1 tsp vanilla extract
175 g/6 oz plain flour
2 tsp ground ginger
1½ tsp bicarbonate of soda
pinch of salt
2 large eggs, lightly beaten
125 ml/4 fl oz milk
whipped cream, to serve

1. Grease the base and sides of an 18-cm/7-inch soufflé dish. Fill the slow cooker with hot (not boiling) water to a depth of about 2.5 cm/1 inch.

2. Put the butter, sugar, golden syrup and vanilla extract into a medium-sized bowl and stir to mix well. Put the flour, ginger, bicarbonate of soda and salt into a large mixing bowl and stir to combine. Stir the butter mixture into the flour mixture with a wooden spoon and mix together until well combined. Add the eggs and milk and continue to mix until smooth.

3. Pour the mixture into the prepared soufflé dish and carefully place it in the slow cooker. Cover and cook on low for about 3 hours until a skewer inserted into the centre of the cake comes out clean. Leave the soufflé dish in the slow cooker pot, remove the pot from the slow cooker base and transfer to a wire rack to cool for at least 30 minutes. Remove the soufflé dish from the pot and leave to cool for a further 30 minutes.

4. To serve, slice the cake into wedges and top with a dollop of whipped cream.

BROWN SUGAR
APPLE CAKE

SERVES: *6–8* | **PREP:** *10 mins, plus cooling* | **COOK:** *2 hours 30 minutes–3 hours*

INGREDIENTS

185 g/6½ oz self-raising flour
½ tsp ground cinnamon
pinch of salt
115 g/4 oz unsalted butter, softened,
  plus extra for greasing
225 g/8 oz soft light brown sugar
2 large eggs, lightly beaten
1 tsp vanilla extract
1 cooking apple, peeled, cored and
  finely diced
whipped cream, to serve

1. Grease the inside of the slow cooker with butter.

2. Sift the flour, cinnamon and salt into a medium-sized bowl. Put the butter and sugar into a large bowl and cream with a hand-held electric mixer.

3. Add the eggs and vanilla extract and beat on high for 1–2 minutes. Fold in the flour mixture using a metal spoon, then gently fold through the diced apple.

4. Spoon the mixture into the prepared slow cooker and level the surface. Cover and cook on low for 2 hours 30 minutes–3 hours, or until the cake is risen, springy to the touch and a skewer inserted into the centre of the cake comes out clean.

5. Remove the slow cooker pot from the base of the slow cooker, transfer to a wire rack and leave to cool for at least 1 hour. Run a flexible palette knife around the outside of the cake and underneath it to release it from the pot, then carefully turn it out onto a serving platter. Serve with a dollop of whipped cream.

CHOCOLATE CAKE

SERVES: *8* | **PREP:** *20 mins, plus cooling* | **COOK:** *2 hours 40 mins, plus standing*

INGREDIENTS

375 g/13 oz plain chocolate, broken
*   into pieces*
175 g/6 oz unsalted butter, plus
*   extra for greasing*
175 g/6 oz light muscovado sugar
4 eggs
2 tsp vanilla extract
150 g/5½ oz self-raising flour
55 g/2 oz ground almonds
125 ml/4 fl oz double cream
icing sugar, for dusting

1. Place a trivet in the base of the slow cooker. Grease and base-line a 20-cm/8-inch diameter deep cake tin, or a cake tin that fits into your slow cooker.

2. Put 250 g/9 oz of the chocolate into a bowl set over a saucepan of gently simmering water and heat until melted. Remove from the heat and cool slightly.

3. Beat the butter and sugar in a large bowl until pale and fluffy. Gradually beat in the eggs. Stir in the melted chocolate and 1 teaspoon of vanilla extract. Evenly fold in the flour and almonds.

4. Spoon the mixture into the prepared tin, spreading evenly. Place in the slow cooker, cover and cook on high for 2½ hours or until risen and springy to the touch.

5. Remove from the slow cooker and leave to cool in the tin for 10 minutes, then turn out onto a wire rack and leave to cool completely.

6. Put the remaining chocolate, the vanilla extract and cream in a saucepan and heat gently, stirring, until melted. Leave to cool until thick enough to spread. Split the cake into two layers and sandwich together with the filling. Dust with icing sugar to serve.

STRAWBERRY CHEESECAKE

SERVES: 6–8 | **PREP:** 20 mins, plus cooling | **COOK:** 2 hours 5 mins, plus standing

INGREDIENTS

85 g/3 oz unsalted butter, melted

140 g/5 oz digestive biscuits, crushed

300 g/10½ oz strawberries, hulled

600 g/1 lb 5 oz full-fat soft cheese

225 g/8 oz caster sugar

2 large eggs, beaten

2 tbsp cornflour

finely grated rind and juice of 1 lemon

1. Stir the butter into the crushed biscuits and press the mixture into the base of a 20-cm/8-inch round springform tin, or a tin that fits into your slow cooker.

2. Purée or mash half the strawberries and whisk together with the cheese, sugar, eggs, cornflour and lemon rind and juice until smooth.

3. Tip the mixture into the tin and place in the slow cooker. Cover and cook on high for about 2 hours, or until almost set.

4. Turn off the slow cooker and leave the cheesecake in the cooker for 2 hours. Remove from the slow cooker and leave in the tin to cool completely, then unclip and release the springform and turn out the cake onto a serving plate.

5. Decorate with the remaining sliced strawberries and serve.

MINI PUMPKIN CHEESECAKES
WITH GINGERNUT CRUST

SERVES: *4* | **PREP:** *20–25 mins, plus cooling & chilling* | **COOK:** *2 hours 10 mins*

INGREDIENTS
BASE

115 g/4 oz gingernut biscuits,
  crushed
2 tbsp soft light brown sugar
pinch of salt
3 tbsp unsalted butter, melted

TOPPING

1 tbsp flour
¼ tsp ground cinnamon
pinch of grated nutmeg
pinch of salt
2 large eggs
100 g/3½ oz soft light brown sugar
115 g/4 oz cream cheese
200 g/7 oz pumpkin purée
2 tbsp double cream
2 tsp vanilla extract
1 tbsp whisky
icing sugar, for dusting

1. To make the base, preheat the oven to 190°C/375°F/Gas Mark 5. Put the crushed gingernuts, sugar and salt into a food processor and pulse several times. Add the butter and pulse until well combined. Press the mixture into the bases and about three quarters of the way up the sides of four 225-ml/8-fl oz ramekins. Place the ramekins on a baking tray and bake in the preheated oven for 10 minutes. Leave to cool.

2. To make the topping, put the flour, cinnamon, nutmeg and salt into a large bowl and whisk together. Whisk in the eggs, sugar, cream cheese, pumpkin purée, cream, vanilla extract and whisky.

3. Spoon the topping into the ramekins and place the ramekins in the slow cooker. Carefully add boiling water to a depth of 4 cm/1½ inches. Cover and cook on high for about 2 hours until the filling is set. Turn off the slow cooker and leave the ramekins inside for a further 1 hour, then remove them from the slow cooker and chill in the refrigerator for at least 2 hours. Dust with icing sugar before serving.

INDEX

Halibut
Ginger-steamed Halibut with Tomatoes & Beans 130
Halibut with Fennel & Olives 128

Ham
Ham Cooked in Cider 86
Jambalaya 152

Kale
Italian Bread Soup with Greens 12
Kale, Quinoa & Cauliflower Soup 82
White Bean Stew 31

Lamb
Lamb with Spring Vegetables 117
Lamb Stew with Artichoke & Rosemary 114
Lamb Tagine 112
Springtime Lamb with Asparagus 111

Leeks
Cock-a-Leekie Soup 50
Salmon with Leeks & Cream 122
Spring Chicken Stew with Chive Dumplings 46
Turkey Breast With Bacon, Leeks & Prunes 77

Lentils: Spaghetti with Lentil Bolognese Sauce 18

Mushrooms
Beef Stew 106
Chicken & Mushroom Stew 53
Chicken Parmigiana 66
Prawn Bisque 139
Sea Bream in Lemon Sauce 137
Turkey & Rice Casserole 74
Vegetable Pasta 23

Nuts
Apple Crumble 165
Chocolate & Walnut Sponge 158
Nutty Chicken 57
Stuffed Apples 173
Tofu with Spicy Peanut Sauce 40

Pasta
Chicken Noodle Soup 51
Macaroni Cheese with Toasted Breadcrumbs 26
Pasta & Prawns 140
Spaghetti with Lentil Bolognese Sauce 18
Sweet & Sour Sicilian Pasta 20
Tagliatelle with Tuna 134
Vegetable Pasta 23

Pearl barley
Lamb with Spring Vegetables 117
Shredded Beef & Pearl Barley Stew 108
Spring Chicken Stew with Chive Dumplings 46

Pears: Blushing Pears 169

Peas
Lamb with Spring Vegetables 117
Red Thai Curry with Salmon & Lime 120
Spring Chicken Stew with Chive Dumplings 46
Tagliatelle with Tuna 134
Vegetable Curry 37

Peppers
Aubergine Timbales 29
Black Bean Chilli with Smoked Chipotle & Red Pepper 8
Chicken Parmigiana 66
Hungarian Pork Goulash 88
Jambalaya 152
Louisiana Courgettes 36
Louisiana Gumbo 144
Mexican Pork Chops 95
Peppers Stuffed with Farro, Feta & Herbs 34
Pollock Bake 132
South-western Seafood Stew 150
Sweet & Sour Sicilian Pasta 20
Vegetarian Paella 42
Pollock Bake 132

Pork
Boston Baked Beans 84
Hungarian Pork Goulash 88
Mexican Pork Chops 95
Pork Stuffed With Apples 87
Sausage & Bean Cassoulet 90
Spicy Pulled Pork 92

Potatoes
Beef Stew 106
Greek Bean & Vegetable Soup 13
New England Clam Chowder 142
Poached Salmon with Dill & Lime 124
Turkey Hash 78

Pumpkins
Mini Pumpkin Cheesecakes with Gingernut Crust 188
Pumpkin Risotto 24

Quinoa
Kale, Quinoa & Cauliflower Soup 82
Stuffed Butternut Squash 14

Rice
Asparagus & Spinach Risotto 25
Jambalaya 152
Mexican Chicken Bowls 48
Prawn Bisque 139
Pumpkin Risotto 24
Rice Pudding 160
Turkey & Rice Casserole 74
Vegetarian Paella 42

Salmon
Poached Salmon with Dill & Lime 124

Red Thai Curry with Salmon & Lime 120
Salmon Florentine 125
Salmon with Leeks & Cream 122
Sausage & Bean Cassoulet 90
Sea Bream in Lemon Sauce 137

Spinach
Asparagus & Spinach Risotto 25
Beef Roulades with Spinach & Feta Cheese 110
Salmon Florentine 125
Tofu with Spicy Peanut Sauce 40

Strawberry Cheesecake 186

Sweet potatoes
Sweet Potato, Apple & Raisin Compote 177
Turkey Chilli with Sweet Potatoes 72
Tofu with Spicy Peanut Sauce 40

Tomatoes
Baked Aubergine with Courgette & Tomato 39
Beef & Chipotle Burritos 102
Bulgarian Chicken 71
Butternut Squash & Goat's Cheese Enchiladas 32
Cavolo Nero, Goat's Cheese & Sun-dried Tomato Frittata 10
Chicken & Mushroom Stew 53
Chicken Cacciatore 62
Chicken Parmigiana 66
Chicken Quesadillas 58
Chipotle Chicken 65
Clams in Spicy Broth with Chorizo 148
Easy Bouillabaisse 147
French-style Fish Stew 127
Ginger-steamed Halibut with Tomatoes & Beans 130
Hungarian Pork Goulash 88
Jambalaya 152
Lamb Stew with Artichoke & Rosemary 114
Lamb Tagine 112
Louisiana Courgettes 36
Pasta & Prawns 140
Seafood in Saffron Sauce 149
South-western Seafood Stew 150
Spaghetti with Lentil Bolognese Sauce 18
Sweet & Sour Sicilian Pasta 20
Turkey Chilli with Sweet Potatoes 72
Vegetable Pasta 23
Vegetarian Paella 42

Turkey
Turkey & Rice Casserole 74
Turkey Breast With Bacon, Leeks & Prunes 77
Turkey Chilli with Sweet Potatoes 72
Turkey Hash 78
Turkey Meatloaf 75

This edition published by Parragon Books Ltd in 2017
LOVE FOOD is an imprint of Parragon Books Ltd

Parragon Books Ltd
Chartist House
15–17 Trim Street
Bath BA1 1HA, UK
www.parragon.com/lovefood

ISBN 978-1-4748-6892-1

Printed in China

Edited by Fiona Biggs
Cover photography by Al Richardson

The cover shot shows the White Bean Stew on page 31.

.... *Notes for the Reader* ....

This book uses both metric and imperial measurements.
Follow the same units of measurement throughout;
do not mix metric and imperial. All spoon measurements
are level: teaspoons are assumed to be 5 ml, and tablespoons
are assumed to be 15 ml. Unless otherwise stated, milk
is assumed to be full fat, eggs and individual fruits and
vegetables are medium, pepper is freshly ground black
pepper and salt is table salt. Unless otherwise stated,
all root vegetables should be peeled prior to using.

The times given are an approximate guide only.
Preparation times differ according to the techniques used
by different people and the cooking times may also vary
from those given.

Vegetarians should be aware that some of the ready-made
ingredients used in the recipes in this book might contain
animal products. Always check the packaging before use.